improving your backgammon

PAUL LAMFORD

and SIMON GASQUOINE

First published in 2002 by Gloucester Publishers plc, (formerly Everyman Publishers plc), Northburgh House, 10 Northburgh Street, London, EC1V 0AT

Reprinted 2003

British Library Cataloguing-in-Publication Data
A catalogue record for this book is available from the British Library.

ISBN 1 85744 315 2

Distributed in North America by The Globe Pequot Press, P.O Box 480, 246 Goose Lane, Guilford, CT 06437-0480.

All other sales enquiries should be directed to Gloucester Publishers plc, Northburgh House, 10 Northburgh Street, London, EC1V 0AT

tel: 020 7253 7887 fax: 020 7490 3708
email: info@everymanchess.com
website: www.everymanchess.com

The Mindsports series was designed and developed by First Rank Publishing

Typest by Games and Pastimes Conultancy, London
Cover design by Horatio Monteverde.
Production by Navigator Guides.

Printed by Lightning Source

Contents

Introduction

The aim of this book is to cover areas of the game in which we have new material to contribute, or themes that have not been considered by other authors. It is not intended to be a comprehensive reference work on all aspects of the game.

We have assumed that all readers are familiar with the basic strategy of the game, and the notation. If not, then a previous book by Lamford, *Starting Out in Backgammon*, also published by Everyman, is an essential preliminary read. This book does not repeat any of the material in that earlier text.

Part One concentrates on money games or positions in which match scores do not play a major factor. From time to time a position will also be discussed in the context of a match situation, in which the answer might be different. There are many original formulas and methods of calculation which have not previously appeared in book form. For example, in Chapter 1, we give our own method of evaluating races, which we believe to be the most accurate available. Readers can compare this with other systems such as the Thorp, Ward or Kleinman methods and choose the one that they find easiest to use. Some of the other material is fairly technical. However, the benefit of learning it can be substantial, and a little effort should reap financial reward in money or tournament play.

The authors gratefully acknowledge the assistance in the preparation of this book of the computer program Snowie. Where appropriate, we have performed rollouts with Snowie 4, released just before we went to press, and the percentage of backgammons, gammons, and wins are given for each side, together with the cubeless equity (or sometimes the cubeful equity). The percentage of wins includes both gammons and backgammons, while the percentage of gammons includes the backgammons, so the cubeless equity can be calculated by adding the figures for one side and subtracting the figures for the other side. Chapter 4 explains equity in more detail. For example, on page 18 we have the following rollout data:

	BG	G	W	L	G	BG	Eq
22/14	0.0%	0.0%	0.1%	99.9%	1.2%	0.0%	−2.02
6/1 5/2	0.0%	0.0%	8.0%	92.0%	19.5%	0.3%	−2.04

The information is presented from the point of view of the player on roll. The cubeless equity can be obtained by adding the backgammons, gammons and wins for White and subtracting those for Black. Thus, for the play 22/14, the cubeless equity is (0.001 − 0.999 − 0.012), or −1.01. This is multiplied by two, the value of the cube, to give a cubeless equity of −2.02. If more relevant, the equity for the appropriate cube position is given, shown in the table as **CEq**, instead of the cubeless equity. Chapter Four also gives valuable practical advice on estimating these equities at the table.

The rollouts have not been relied upon without scrutiny, and in some cases the authors are convinced that Snowie does not understand a particular position.The top German player Johannes Leverman has indicated that Snowie 4 has made a further breakthrough in conceptual understanding but there were no major differences in its evaluations of the positions in this book.

Simon Gasquoine, who assisted Paul Lamford with several previous books, wrote most of Part Two of the book, in particular the explanation of both basic and advanced concepts in match play. His gammon chart on page 101, compiled from my match equity program, is an invaluable shortcut to assist the player more familiar with money games in understanding the importance of gammons at different scores. In this part of the book the match score appears in parenthesis next to the words WHITE and BLACK in the diagrams.

Stefanie Rohan researched all the internet sites and computer software. There are many new servers offering both match and money play and she has appraised the main sites and their pluses and minuses. A summary of the backgammon software and a list of suppliers should be of use.

Both Simon and Stefanie made invaluable suggestions and improvements throughout the book. Byron Jacobs again provided excellent support in the production and preparation of this book. The authors accept responsibility for any errors and would welcome comments sent to them at gampas@aol.com.

We have adopted the convention of referring to White, or 'the player' as 'he' and Black, or 'the opponent', as 'she'.

Paul Lamford, London, October 2002

Part One

Money Games

by Paul Lamford

Chapter One

The Race

- **Borderline Doubles**
- **Marginal Takes**
- **A Race Formula**
- **Cube Ownership**
- **Short Races**
- **Efficiency**

This chapter deals with the race — any position in which contact has been broken. The rules for offering and taking cubes are fairly well defined, and several formulas exist which allow us to calculate winning chances accurately. We shall concentrate on positions in which one or both sides have eight checkers or more. Positions with fewer checkers are adequately covered in other textbooks. We shall start by considering the minimum advantage needed to double.

Borderline Doubles

It is almost impossible to lose a gammon in a "pure" race, although the author managed to do so once, without a checker being hit, after each sides had rolled two opening 6-5s running both back checkers to the respective mid-points!

The rule in *Starting Out in Backgammon* of doubling with a 10% advantage and taking with a 12½% disadvantage is a good general guide which loses little. For medium and short races we can adjust these figures slightly:

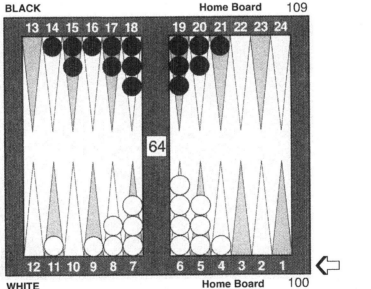

Diag. 1

With an advantage of exactly 9% of his own pip-count, White has a marginal double. The equity is +0.72 with the cube centred and +0.73 with the cube on Black's side. Increase the race length or decrease the lead and it would be wrong to double. Decrease the race length and we can double with a smaller percentage advantage.

Marginal Takes

The next diagram is a borderline take/pass with a race deficit of 13% and a cube-owned equity of –0.99:

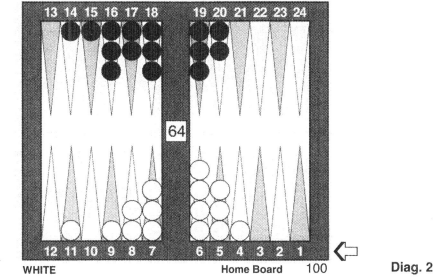

Diag. 2

Any decrease in the race length, while maintaining the same percentage advantage, would make this a clear pass. Increasing the race length would make it a clear take.

A Race Formula

In a money game, the above rules are adequate for deciding whether we should double and whether we should take. However, at a particular match score, a money take may become a pass (or even no double), and we therefore need to make an accurate estimate of the winning chances. For example, if we are leading 8-5 in an 11-point match and own a 2-cube in a race, we need to perform two calculations in order to decide whether to double and whether to accept a double:

a) To work out the doubling window as described in Chapter 5.

b) To estimate the winning chances to the nearest percentage.

This section is concerned primarily with making an accurate estimate of the winning chances in a race. We are fortunate to be living in the computer age, and the strongest backgammon programs are able to roll out positions a large number of times in order to accurately estimate the winning chances in any position. The following chart, derived from rollouts, gives the approximate winning chances in races of different lengths.

Roller's Pips	Pip Lead for Roller						
	0	*5*	*10*	*15*	*20*	*25*	*30*
20	70%	81%	91%	96%	98%	99%	99%
40	65%	76%	85%	92%	95%	97%	98%
60	62%	72%	80%	87%	92%	95%	97%
80	60%	68%	77%	86%	91%	94%	95%
100	58%	67%	76%	83%	87%	91%	94%
120	57%	67%	76%	82%	86%	89%	93%

Remembering this chart is not easy, but there is a reasonably accurate formula which we can use at the table to estimate the winning chances. It is

$$P = 50\% + \frac{900 + R + 400L}{R + 7L + 25}\%$$

where P is the winning percentage, R is the race length of the leader and L is the lead, adjusted for distributional features.

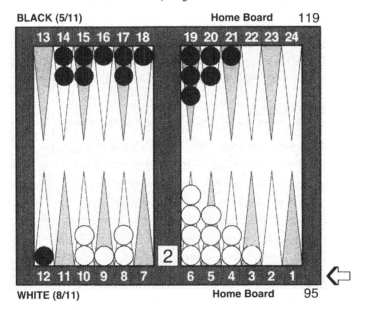

BLACK (5/11)   Home Board   119

WHITE (8/11)   Home Board   95   **Diag. 3**

In the above position, the race length is 95 and the lead is 24, which gives P = 87%. We expect one additional crossover for each 5 pips of lead, so we add a penalty of half a pip per crossover only when they exceed that. Here Black trails by 24 pips and has five more crossovers, so no penalty. A long rollout produced a result of just over 88%. The formula is slightly improved on one we published in the magazine *BIBAFax*.

Of course, we need to be able to work out what this estimate of 87% means to our cube decision, and we will look in Part Two of the book at how to use our newly-gleaned information. A long rollout confirmed the borderline double at the score.

Cube Ownership

How valuable is the doubling cube in a race? One might think that it was less valuable than in a volatile position where both sides are blitzing, but this is not the case. In a race, the advantage changes hands less often and the doubling cube usually confers about **one sixth extra wins on a player with access to the cube**. After we calculate the winning chances using the formula on the previous page, we can add a further one sixth to that figure if we are accepting a cube, or one sixth of the **difference** between our winning percentage and our opponent's if the cube is centred. The following is a good example:

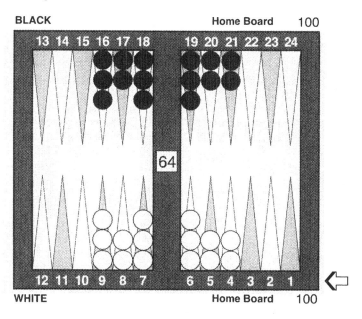

Diag. 4

If we use our formula for White on roll in a race with a lead of 0 and a race length of 100, we get P = 50% + 1000/125 = 58%. Amazingly, a long rollout showed White winning 58.0% of the time (the formula is not normally quite that accurate). This is a useful benchmark position. (Another example worth noting is a race of 50 v 50 in which the player on roll is about 63%.)

Because White is on roll, he is more likely to use the cube first, and we can get close to his **cubeful** winning percentage by adding to his winning chances one sixth of the difference between his winning percentage and that of his opponent. This gives a cubeful figure of 58% + (58% − 42%)/6 = 61% effective wins. If Black owns the cube, she could add one sixth to her 42% wins, giving herself 7% extra wins by virtue of her access to the cube, making her close to even money. These extra wins take two forms, those in which Black gets to double White out, for example after rolling a winning high double, and those in which Black gets to redouble but White has a correct take.

The position is almost a beaver for money, but this would require that Black had positive equity owning the cube, which is not quite the case.

Short Races

As the race decreases in length, positional factors such as efficiency, gaps, wastage and extra checkers acquire an increased significance. We need a set of rules for positions with all checkers in the home boards, as the pip-count on its own is insufficient. An instructive position is the following:

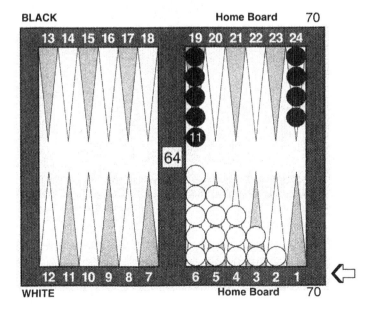

Diag. 5

Despite the equal pip-count, not only does White have a double, but Black has a clear pass. White wins the game 80% of the time. To arrive at this figure we need to adjust the pip-count:

a) For each additional checker on the board add two pips to that player's pip-count.

b) For each checker above two on the ace-point, add two pips; for each checker above two on the deuce-point, add one pip. If there are more than five checkers on any other point, add one pip, but not if you are also adding a penalty for gaps.

c) For a gap on the four-point add four pips. For a gap on the five-point add three pips, for a gap on the three-point add two pips; and for a gap on the two-point add one pip.

d) If there is a gap, but rolling the number corresponding to the gap allows another gap to be filled, the penalty is reduced by around one pip. Judgement should be used here; the largest benefits are when a heavy point is being unstacked.

So we add two pips to Black's count for each checker above two on the ace-point. In addition, Black is penalised four pips for the 4-gap, three pips for the 5-gap, two pips for the 3-gap and one pip for the 2-gap. The total penalty is 14 pips, giving an adjusted race of 70-84. However, we need to look at numbers that fill a gap, and add back one pip for each of those. Black's fives are terrible, but her fours, threes and twos all fill a gap, so we add back three pips for Black, giving an adjusted count of 70-81. Applying our formula we get the following result:

$$50 + (900 + 70 + 4400)/(70 + 77 + 25) = 81\%.$$

Close enough.

Efficiency

As the last diagram shows, distribution of checkers is important. A further factor is the efficiency of the position. We referred to the wastage when a player has more than two checkers on the ace-point, and gave him a two-pip penalty for each surplus checker. However, when either player has **more than six checkers on the lower three points**, he will have general wastage in that he has a large number of checkers with a low pip-count. It is wrong in these cases to add a penalty just for the ace and deuce-points. White's position in Diagram 5 is known as the 'Golden Triangle'. It represents the ideal distribution for a pip-count of 70 for 15 checkers, an average of $4^2/_3$ pips per checker. When a player has an average below that, there is inefficiency, and a penalty based on the difference from the average should be added. For example, with four checkers on each of the one and two points, the average is $1^1/_2$, so the difference is $3^1/_6$. Divide the number of checkers remaining by four (the constant that seems to work best) and multiply by the inefficiency factor to get the appropriate penalty.

However, a benefit of inefficiency is that more doubles work for the player with the stacked position. After applying the penalty, deduct half a pip for each double that bears off four checkers, or bears off three checkers and is likely to save a roll.

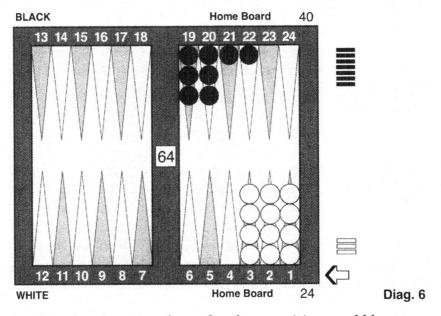

Diag. 6

Based on the pip-count alone, the above position would be a double and a big pass, but White's position is clearly inefficient. To White's pip-count we add:

a) 8 pips for the four extra checkers.

b) White's average pips per checker is only 2. That is $2^2/_3$ below the maximum efficiency average of $4^2/_3$. White has 12 checkers, and we therefore add to White's pip-count (12/4 = 3) times the penalty of $2^2/_3$, a total of 8 pips.

c) We deduct three pips from White's pip-count and half a pip from Black's pip-count for working doubles, as all doubles bear off four checkers for White, whereas only 6-6 does so for Black.

Note that we do not also add pips for the extra checkers on the ace- and deuce-points. That adjustment is already built in.

We thus get an adjusted pip count as follows:

White: $24 + 8 + 8 - 3 = 37$ pips; Black $= 40 - 1/2 = 39\frac{1}{2}$ pips

Our formula now gives the winning chances for the adjusted race of 37-39½ as $50\% + (900 + 37 + 1000)/(37 + 17.5 + 25) = 74\%$. The actual database figure for this position is 74.6% and this confirms the cube action of Double/Take.

This is another position in which adjustments are needed:

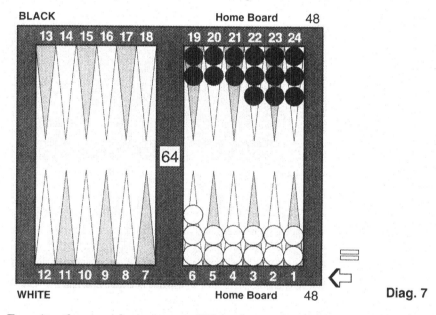

Diag. 7

Despite the equal pip-count, White has a big advantage. We add four pips to Black's pip-count for the extra two checkers. Next we calculate the average pips per checker. Black's average is $48/15 = 3.2$. White's average is $48/13 = 3.7$.

We deduct this average from 4.7, which is our maximum efficiency average. We thus add 1.5 pips to Black for each set of 4 checkers, a total of 5.6. To White we add 1 pip for each set of 4 checkers, a total of 3.3. The adjusted pip count is therefore 51.3 against 57.6. Our formula gives:

$$50\% + (900 + 51 + 2520)/(51 + 44 + 25) = 78.9\%.$$

A borderline pass. A long rollout of the position had White winning 78.4% of the time — a pleasingly accurate result.

Exercise 1: Use the race formula to estimate the winning chances in the position below. As we will see in Chapter 5, Black, who leads 2-1 in a 5-point match, should accept a 4-cube if he is winning 40% of the time. Is it a redouble — and if so, can Black take?

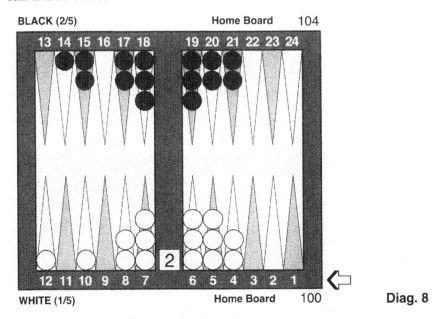

Diag. 8

Exercise 2: This time a money game; adjust the pip-count for gaps and wastage and then decide on the cube action.

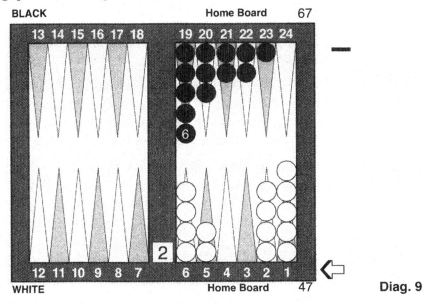

Diag. 9

Chapter Two

Technical Themes

- **Stay or Go?**
- **Hit or Ignore?**
- **Slot or Not?**
- **Extra Shot?**
- **Clear or Hold?**
- **Safe or Bold?**

The headings in this chapter, Stay or Go, Hit or Ignore, Slot or Not, Extra Shot, Clear or Hold, Safe or Bold, are unlikely to win a poetry prize. They do, however, cover the uncertainties which occur in different situations where it would be nice to have general rules or guidelines. I suspect that many of us wonder what is right at the time the problem occurs and then forgot about it when the game is over. We start with a common problem. Should we hang around and wait for that last-ditch shot … or will it just get us gammoned?

Stay or Go?

We form a six-prime on our side of the board, but the shot never seems to come; or one comes but we miss it. How long can we wait for another? Take this position:

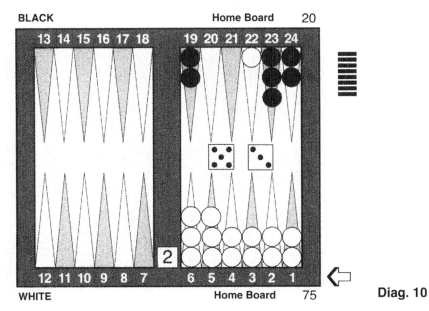

Diag. 10

The decision is whether to stay back, with an increased chance of being gammoned, or to run now and give up on winning the game. For it to be right to stay, we will need to gain half as many wins as we sustain gammon losses. It transpires that the two plays are almost identical in equity:

	BG	G	W	L	G	BG	Eq
22/14:	0.0%	0.0%	0.1%	99.9%	1.2%	0.0%	−2.02
6/1 5/2	0.0%	0.0%	8.0%	92.0%	19.5%	0.3%	−2.04

Although running comes out ahead on cubeless equity (the figure in the last column), if the cube is in play, staying just shades it, as White gets to redouble some of the games in which he hits a checker. The difference is, however, negligible, and another recount in Florida might well change the decision. It might seem we are talking about small errors here and the margin in the above diagram is sufficiently small to make it an ideal benchmark position. However, if we add or remove a black checker then one or the other of the plays becomes a blunder:

In Diagram 11, staying is a huge blunder, losing 0.24 on a 2-cube. The 8% wins are dwarfed by the 30% extra gammons that hanging around costs. Even if we hit we will only be around 20% to win.

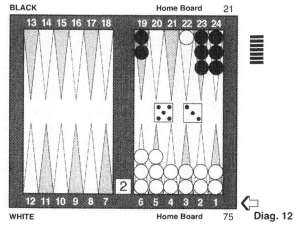

BLACK · Home Board · 18 · WHITE · Home Board · 75 · Diag. 11

In Diagram 12 it is nearly as big a blunder to run, costing 0.21. White is only getting gammoned around 5% by staying and he wins more than that by hitting a shot. This time hitting is over 30% to win, plus an extra 5% because we own the cube.

BLACK · Home Board · 21 · WHITE · Home Board · 75 · Diag. 12

How do we decide whether to run or stay? Quite simply, if we are in gammon danger it is usually right to go; our winning chances will probably be in the 5% range; anything more than 10% in gammons and we should get the hell out of there. Also, if our opponent has the cube, the late shot may not win anyway

— she may have a cash after we hit; so we shouldn't try to win a game that is already lost! One other point — if we are going to get gammoned anyway then we should stay! We must take care not to be backgammoned, however. A couple of sudden doubles when we are stuck in her board can be fatal.

Hit or Ignore?

Usually it is correct to hit in our board when the opponent has just one checker back, but many factors need to be considered:

a) The strength of the opponent's board.

b) The race if we play safe.

c) The location of the cube and whether we can use it effectively.

d) The gammons for each side.

In addition, there could be match score considerations which require that the relative importance of gammons need to be considered. Tough game, backgammon!

Again we start with a benchmark position:

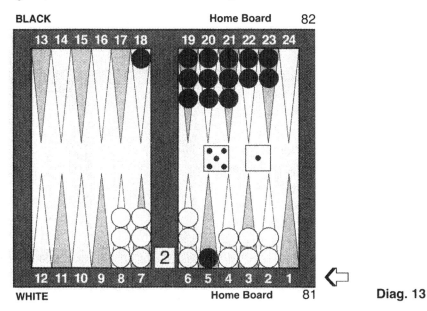

Diag. 13

The basic guideline in this type of position is to hit if we are ahead by less than 10% of our own pip-count after our roll. Here White leads 81-82, but has rolled only six pips, and so leads by only seven. It is better, by a small margin, for White to hit loose, as the rollouts confirmed:

	BG	G	W	L	G	BG	Eq
8/3 6/5*	0.1%	2.1%	57.8%	42.2%	6.0%	0.2%	0.70
7/1	0.0%	0.6%	56.0%	44.0%	0.5%	0.1%	0.67

There is a general rule that we should aim for a race when owning the cube. However, when the race is close, we have to weigh up the risks of hitting against the chances of losing the race. If we are hitting loose, there will be a minimum of 11 and often as many as 15 potentially winning returns. Even a tiny race lead may therefore be preferable, particularly if we own the cube. Just a few pips can dramatically change the decision:

In Diagram 14 it is a massive blunder to play safe. 7/1 loses 0.26 over the correct 8/3 6/5* and would be an even bigger error at double match point. Even if the opponent needed four points in a match, it would be right to hit!

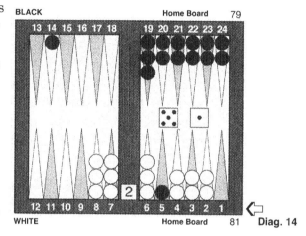

Diag. 14

An even bigger potential error the other way in Diagram 15, in which 8/3 6/5* loses a whopping 0.32 against the correct 7/1. The safe play would also be right if gammons were irrelevant, such as at DMP.

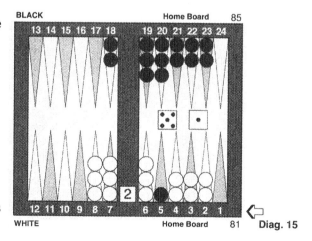

Diag. 15

The above diagrams all show money games in which we own the cube. At different match scores or for different cube positions, we might play differently.

Slot or Not?

A common problem after we have hit a late shot is whether to slot the sixth home-board point when the opponent has a checker on the bar. The decision is often very tough, and we need some general guidelines to help us:

a) The strength of the opponent's board. It is never right to slot against a six-point board and rarely correct against a five-point board. When the opponent has a four-point board the decision is close; but against weaker boards it is usually right to slot.

b) The position of the cube. If the opponent owns the cube it is usually wrong to slot, as we will still need to cover. If we own the cube, then slotting is better, as we may be able to use the cube effectively either before or after covering.

c) The number of checkers the opponent has borne off. The more she has removed, the more inclined we should be to slot, as we will need the close-out to win. If she has only a few checkers borne off, we may win without ever making the sixth point.

d) Which point is open. We should be more inclined to slot a high point, as we usually need to make it to win.

Let us look at how to apply these rules in practice:

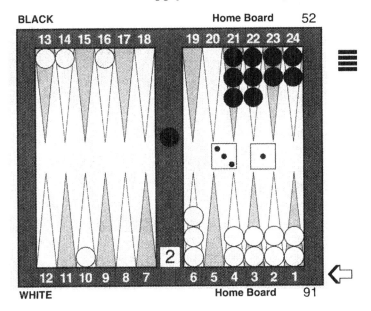

Diag. 16

The power of the cube comes into play here. If White closes out Black, then he will be able to cash the game, and indeed White will often be able to double when the slot is missed. The downside of course is that Black's 11 shots will give her a bundle of gammons. It turns out that slotting and bringing builders down are equally good, at least for money:

	BG	**G**	**W**	**L**	**G**	**BG**	**CEq**
14/11 6/5	0.0%	0.0%	61.1%	38.9%	19.6%	1.2%	0.68
14/11 13/12	0.0%	0.0%	59.1%	40.9%	8.1%	0.3%	0.67

The final equity figure this time is the **cube-centred** figure. If the opponent owned the cube, slotting would be a big error, as we would have to play the game to the end.

In Diagram 17 Black's board is weaker, but she will have a take even after being closed out, as she already has five checkers off. However, White will still get some strong doubles, and slotting is correct by the narrow margin of 0.03.

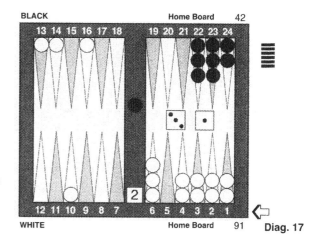

Diag. 17

Black has borne off two fewer checkers than in Diagram 16, and now White may win without making the five-point. If White has access to the cube, 14/11 6/5 is an error by 0.05 and flooding the outfield with 14/11 16/15 is correct, aiming to contain the black checker.

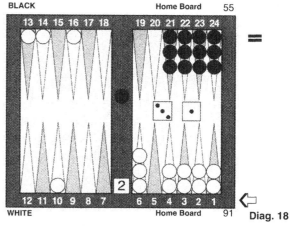

Diag. 18

Extra Shot?

A common problem in the bear-off is whether to remove one or more additional checkers at the cost of one or more extra shots. A typical choice is whether to leave 11 or 12 shots:

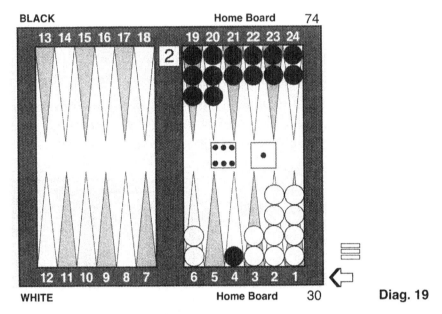

Diag. 19

In the above position White can remove two checkers with 6/o 5/o, leaving 12 shots, or play 6/o 6/5, giving 11 shots. The factors which influence that choice are as follows:

a) If there are significant gammons, and they are of value, it is often right to bear off even at the cost of two extra shots.

b) If we will get doubled out after being hit, and gammons are negligible, we should minimise shots.

c) The situation can change completely if the opponent has a broken prime or weak board.

When the above factors do not clearly point in one direction, the average player is at **sixes and sevens** whether to bear off the extra checker. This helps us remember our rule for when the opponent has a closed board:

If we can get a **sixth** checker off, we can leave one extra shot; if we can get a **seventh** checker off we can leave two extra shots.

In our position above, White can only get a fifth checker off, so should minimise shots by 6/o 6/5, as the rollouts show:

	BG	G	W	L	G	BG	CEq
6/o 6/5	0.0%	0.1%	74.6%	25.4%	0.0%	0.2%	0.77
6/o 1/o	0.0%	0.2%	74.5%	25.5%	0.0%	0.0%	0.73

The end column is the cube-centred equity and shows the advantage of the safer play. Black is likely to win after any hit.

Change the position a little, so that White can bear a sixth checker off, and it is correct to give an extra shot:

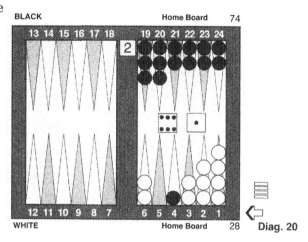

In Diagram 20, the right play is 6/o 1/o on the '**rule of six**'. Although this leaves 12 shots instead of 11, the gain if we do get hit from having borne off one additional checker more than compensates. The play is 0.08 better than 6/o 6/5.

To leave two extra shots, we need to take a seventh checker off and the reason is mainly the extra gammons that we can win, even though the opponent has only one checker to bring home:

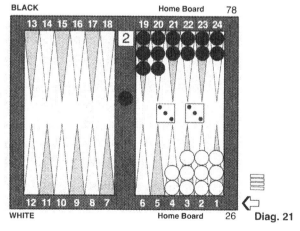

White has to leave a shot here, but the right play is 4/1 3/o (3) leaving 13 shots instead of 11. On the '**rule of seven**', White should take a seventh checker off. This gains 5% gammons and only costs about 1% single wins, with a big gain of 0.09 in money equity. Minimising shots is correct at double match point, when we should play 4/1(2) 3/o(2).

Clear or Hold?

Another tricky decision we may have to make when bearing in against an anchor is whether to clear a point, or maintain a prime with the idea of causing the opposing board to break. We start as ever with a benchmark position:

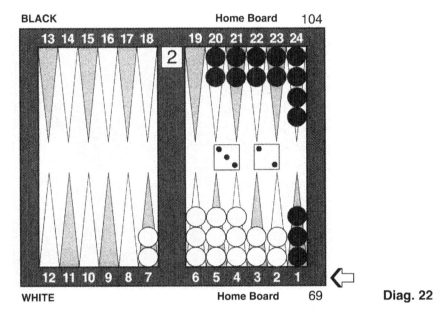

Diag. 22

Black is on the brink of crashing in Diagram 22 and she is very likely to lose another point next roll. Still, it is only a fraction better to hold the prime for one further roll:

	BG	G	W	L	G	BG	Eq
6/3 4/2	0.1%	34.0%	95.5%	4.5%	0.0%	0.2%	2.52
7/5 7/6	1.7%	31.8%	96.1%	3.9%	0.0%	0.0%	2.49

The final column is the cubeful value, and it can be seen that clearing the bar-point is correct at double match point. With the cube in play, however, Black is much more likely to get an effective redouble if she can keep her board intact, and if she pops a six and gets an early shot, a strong board will be critical.

What are the most important criteria for deciding whether to clear the back of the prime?

a) Whether we can force the opponent to bury a third or fourth checker. This will make it harder or even impossible for her to close us out.

b) Clearing the bar is much more important than clearing our six-point. If we blot on the bar when we are bearing in, we can still be gammoned; if we blot on our six-point, we will be bearing off in the process, so we will not be gammoned.

c) The number of spare pips our opponent has is critical, as are the numbers which she cannot play. Sometimes our opponent will get an unplayable six or five with a playable small number and thus avoid crashing.

In Diagram 23, even though our opponent has no spare pips, clearing the bar with 7/4 7/5 is 0.13 better than 6/3 4/2. After the latter, Black will still usually have a five-prime next roll, and there are five blotting numbers to boot.

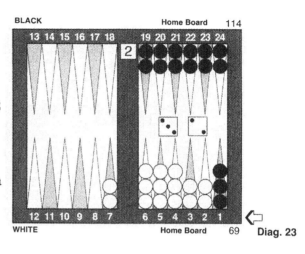

If we have already cleared the bar, as in Diagram 24, we usually do better to keep a five-prime if our opponent is about to crash. Here it is marginally correct to clear the six-point at double match point, but in a money game it is 0.10 better to play 5/4 2/o. This increases gammons from 30% to 36%, and makes it much more likely that Black's board will

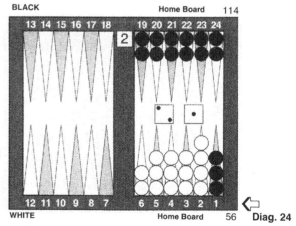

crash, at the cost of some horror rolls like 6-5 next time. Black would prefer that the checkers on her ace-point were further back.

Safe or Bold?

An excellent chapter in Magriel's *Backgammon* discusses when to play aggressively and when to exercise prudence. The book is worth buying (from a supplier on page 113 or from ebay) for this section alone. We often have a choice between a safe play, maybe leaving no shots but conceding a positional asset, or a bold play, trying to achieve our aims but perhaps leaving half a dozen shots.

In the following position White is trying to contain a solitary black checker; hitting is mandatory, but should White leave the bar slotted?

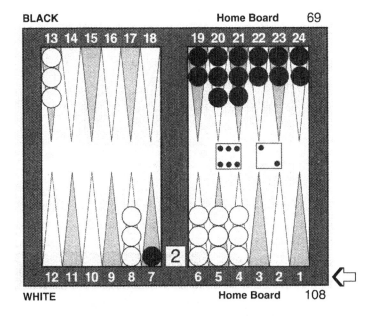

Diag. 25

White would very much like to make the bar, but the six shots that leaving it slotted entails are a big price. As we might expect by now, lifting and leaving arc too close to call:

	BG	G	W	L	G	BG	Eq
13/7*5	0.1%	1.9%	58.5%	41.5%	3.7%	0.1%	0.38
13/7* 13/11	0.2%	2.0%	61.1%	38.9%	14.9%	0.3%	0.37

The half-hearted attempt to guard against gammons while still keeping the bar slotted, 13/7* 8/6, is much worse. We significantly reduce the number of rolls that make a five-prime and also run the same immediate risk.

What are the features that dictate whether we should make a bold play or go for safety?

a) **The strength of the opponent's board**. If the opponent has a closed board, being hit is usually fatal. Even one point open could make a difference.

b) **The gammon threat**. If a loose play distributes blots like confetti at a wedding, this will increase the danger of being gammoned when things go wrong.

c) **How much one gains from the bold play if it comes off**. If we are losing even after some exotic double slot gets missed, then such a bold play is probably wrong.

In Diagram 26, Black has only a 5-point board, and this gives White five returns if Black hits on White's bar. This makes 13/7* 13/11 better by 0.05 and hugely better at double match point.

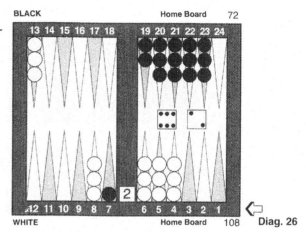

In Diagram 27, Black's position is even stronger if she hits a fly-shot, as she will have time to pick up further checkers. 13/7*/5 now gets the nod by the same margin of 0.05. One factor in such positions is the race. If we decrease the race deficit, this increases our tendency to play safe, as there is then a second way to win.

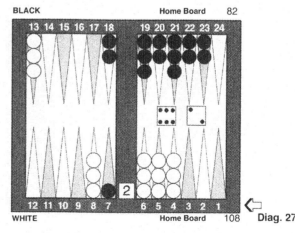

Exercise 3: White seems to be in trouble in the next diagram; how would you play in a money game, and what would you do at a score such as 2 away/4 away, where gammons are very valuable to your opponent?

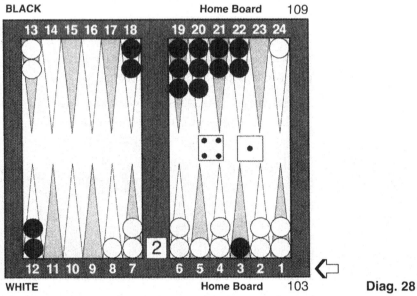

Diag. 28

Exercise 4: How would you play here in a money game; and would it make any difference if the situation were 9-9 in an 11-point match, in effect double match point?

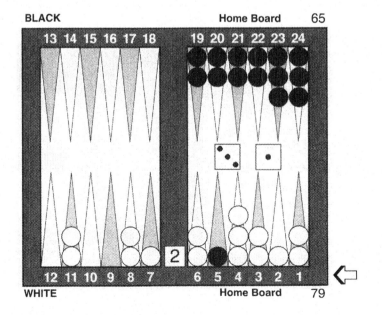

Diag. 29

Chapter Three

Blitzes

A blitz is an attempt to close out one or more opposing checkers. The play is essentially tactical and the cube decisions are difficult. This chapter will attempt to provide some benchmark positions for both cube and checker play.

Critical Features

Let us start with a typical blitz and look at the factors that will influence the cube decision for each side:

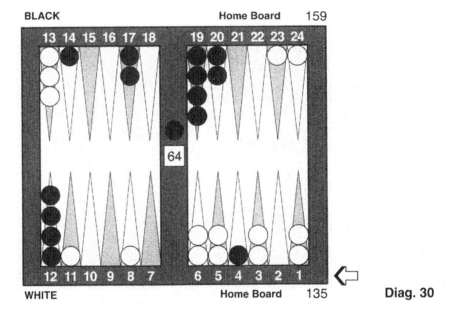

Diag. 30

Black has been caught without a defensive anchor, and it is clear that White has a powerful double, whether in a money game or early in a long match. Black has a borderline take, as the rollouts show:

BG	G	W	L	G	BG	Eq
2.1%	41.1%	65.3%	34.7%	9.4%	0.7%	0.64

The end figure is White's cubeless equity. If we roll out the position with Black owning a 2-cube, she has an equity of −0.94, so Black has a clear take. The reason for this is that she gets some powerful redoubles if she anchors. Because she is winning a lot of games, in many of which she will have an opportunity to redouble, she is able to accept a cube with a lower negative cubeless equity than normal.

What are the critical features of the position?

a) Perhaps the most important aspect of a blitz is the number of opposing checkers on the bar. If the black checker on her 21-point were on the bar, then she would have to pass. If the checker on the bar were on Black's 23-point, then White would not have a double.

b) The number of points White has made in board. If we move the checkers on White's ace-point back to his eight-point, then he has only a borderline double. Move two checkers from his mid-point to his deuce-point and he is even Too Good to Double.

c) The direct hitters. If the checker on White's 11-point were moved to his 10-point, Black would have to pass. If White's builder on his eight-point were moved back to his mid-point, then the double would be marginal, although still correct.

d) The compensation on Black's side of the board. If Black did not have her five-point, she would have a big pass. If Black also had her four-point she would have an easy take, although White would still have a clear double.

e) Whether the blitzer has split or escaped his back checkers. Here White has split, which is beneficial. Black would have an easier take if he hadn't. Move White's checker on his 23-point to his mid-point and Black has a big pass again. Even if she anchors, her opponent may easily win the race by escaping the remaining checker.

f) Whether there are loose checkers to be picked up. If the Black checker on the 11-point were back on her mid-point, this would favour Black, but it would still be a clear double. If a checker on the mid-point were on her nine-point, then Black would have to pass. The threat of having further checkers sent to the bar is too strong.

g) The race, as ever, has some importance. Move a checker from Black's six-point back to her mid-point and she has to pass. Instead move a checker from Black's mid-point to her eight-point and the take is easier.

New Point or Hit

Whether to make a new inner-board point or to hit another checker when conducting a blitz is sometimes a tough decision. The general rule is that hitting on the four-point or five-point takes priority over making a new inner-board point, but hitting on the deuce-point or ace-point does not. Hitting on the three-point or making a new inner-board point will be a close decision. In the following position White has such a choice:

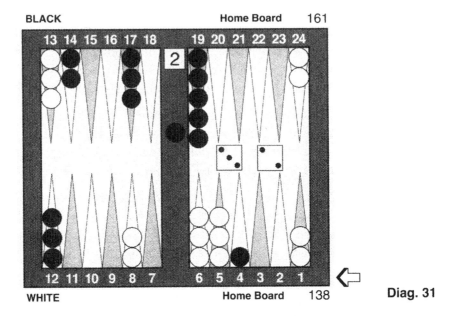

Diag. 31

White does better here to hit with 6/4* 13/10 (0.02 better than 6/4* 24/21). Making the three-point loses around 0.08. Black's board is weak, and making a fourth point takes away a couple of builders. If we make the three-point and Black pops a four, she gets a good game.

Change the position slightly and it is still correct to hit on the four-point, but Black's stronger forward position means that it is now right for White to split at the back. In many positions the best play combines offence and defence, and doing something on both sides of the board

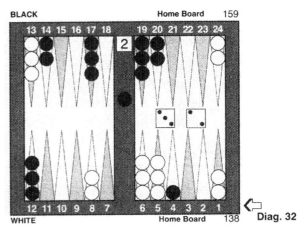

Diag. 32

must always be considered. If Black does anchor we will then be poised to make an advanced anchor ourselves.

If the choice is between hitting on the deuce-point or making the three-point, then the latter is better. In diagram 33, 6/3 5/3 is correct. If Black then rolls a deuce, she only makes a low anchor, which is not as strong as a high anchor.

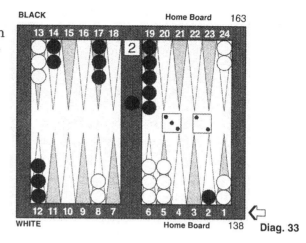

Diag. 33

Switching

We define a switch as a move, after rolling a double, of two checkers from an occupied home-board point to another home-board point occupied by an opposing checker. In general, a switch is correct, as it buys some time to continue the blitz. The close decisions come when we have a six-prime and do not necessarily want our opponent to stay on the bar:

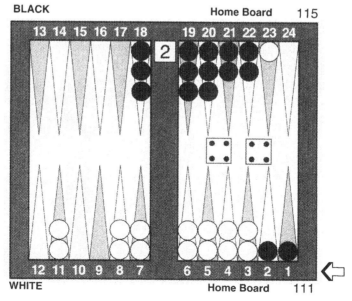

Diag. 34

In the preceding position, the Snowie 3-ply evaluation favours 11/3(2) by a full third of a point over the switching play of 6/2*(2) 5/1*(2). This would make the switching play a whopping blunder, but the rollouts paint a different picture:

	BG	G	W	L	G	BG	Eq
6/2*(2) 5/1* (2)	0.5%	24.9%	66.1%	33.9%	6.1%	0.2%	0.42
11/3 (2)	0.8%	15.8%	65.9%	34.1%	8.7%	0.3%	0.29

Switching wins more gammons, with no decrease in the number of wins, and is correct even at double match point. The point is that Black can keep her five-prime next turn without having to hit on the two-point (unless she rolls 5-5, 4-4 or 3-3). Stacking the two spares on the three-point makes it more difficult to attack if White's next roll does not contain a six.

When is switching correct?

a) If it increases the number of gammons, and they count.

b) If it buys time to escape a back checker by putting one or more opposing checkers on the bar.

c) To stop the opponent attacking us by taking away half or all her roll.

d) When the alternative leads to an awkward stacked position.

Switching is wrong if the priority is to allow the opponent's prime to crash. A seemingly small change to the above position alters the play considerably, as the next two diagrams show:

In Diagram 35, White can distribute his spares much more efficiently, and 12/4 11/3 is correct by 0.07. Even if White does not get a six next roll, he will be well-placed to attack or point on the ace- or deuce-point, buying more time to escape. He can hit loose instead if necessary.

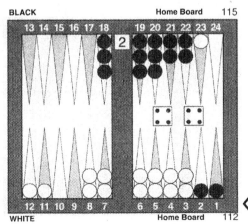

Diag. 35

Changing the position by moving a checker from Black's bar-point to her four-point makes it correct now to keep the six-prime. Black will be forced to break her five-prime with all sixes and all the medium doubles.

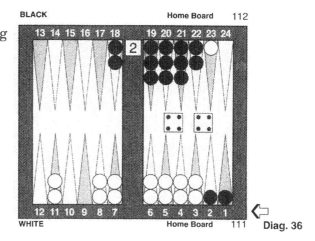

In Diagram 36, 11/4(2) is correct by 0.12.

Anchor Away

We have all been there. We survive the first wave of the blitz and get an anchor with a lucky double. Later we have a chance to hit a shot. We might not get another one, we reason, and choose to hit. The opponent hits back from the bar and we get gammoned anyway. The following position is instructive:

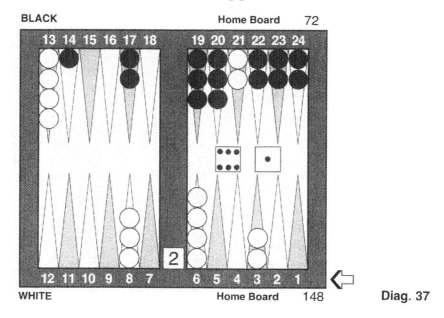

Should White hit and risk a gammon, or should he wimp out? Rollouts show that the decision is very close:

	BG	**G**	**W**	**L**	**G**	**BG**	**CEq**
21/14*	0.1%	1.3%	19.0%	81.0%	44.6%	0.8%	-1.00
13/7 8/7	0.0%	0.5%	10.2%	89.8%	25.7%	0.2%	-1.01

The end figure is the cubeful equity, and the cubeless rollouts also make the decision too close to call. What factors influence our choice?

a) The strength of the opponent's board. Move the two checkers on Black's ace-point to her two-point and three-point and it is a blunder not to hit.

b) The strength of our board; move the checkers on White's three-point to his six-point and now it is a blunder to hit.

c) The number of returns. Here Black gets 15 returns from the bar, and they are potential gammons. An increase in this figure would suggest playing safe. A decrease would tempt us to hit.

d) Whether we are likely to get gammoned anyway. Here White has 17 crossovers to save the gammon, while Black needs 18 crossovers to bear off all the checkers, so White may still get gammoned if he doesn't hit. Move two checkers from White's mid-point to his six-point and it would be wrong to hit.

e) Which point we are hitting from. If we are likely to escape should we survive the potential returns, we should tend to hit; if we still have work to do to escape, we should play safe.

Even small modifications can radically change the decision.

Here White has his five-point and is better-placed to contain the black checker. It is now a huge error not to hit, losing 0.23. In addition, the number of returns from the bar has been reduced to 13, as there is some duplication of ones, twos and fours.

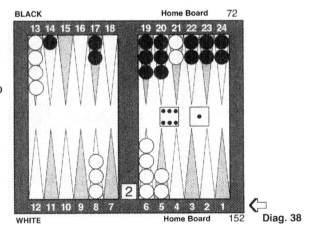

Diag. 38

If White has the
ace-point instead
of the five-point,
then it is a large
error to hit, losing
0.08. The
combination of
White's eight-point
and ace-point is
particularly
ineffective for
constraining the
black checker that

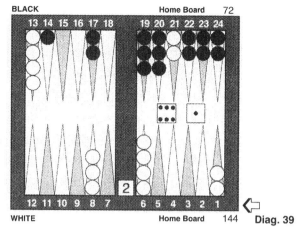

Diag. 39

we hit, and Black will hit on her four-point with impunity.

Redoubling

A blitz is a very committal strategy; when things go wrong the
advantage can change hands rapidly. Usually, but not always,
the person conducting the blitz is ahead in the race.

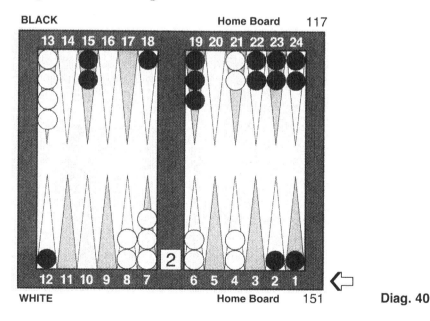

Diag. 40

Black has just rolled an unfortunate six when entering from
the bar, and now White should consider a redouble. Black has a
failed blitz with the checkers on her lower points out of play,
but she has a race lead and a stronger board, so that a later hit

could easily revive the attack. The rollout results are interesting:

BG	G	W	L	G	BG	CEq
0.9%	20.0%	68.3%	31.7%	9.7%	0.3%	1.44

The last column is the equity on a 4-cube after redoubling. The cube-owned equity (on a 2-cube) is virtually the same (1.46), making the redouble marginally wrong, but justified if there is the slightest chance our opponent will hallucinate and pass.

No chance of that, we might think, but a small change to the position gives Black a borderline pass. White now has his five-point instead of his four-point, and this makes it a lot easier to extend the prime and contain any black checkers that are hit. The equity here is 2.02 on a 4-cube, which makes it another useful benchmark position.

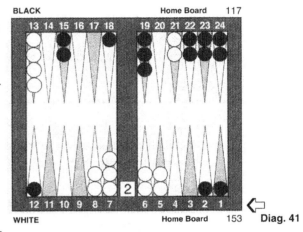

Diag. 41

Move the two checkers on the five-point back to White's six-point and it becomes hugely wrong to double, losing 0.66 on a 4-cube! Even if White hits one of the two loose checkers in the outfield, Black is very likely to make a high anchor with her reply.

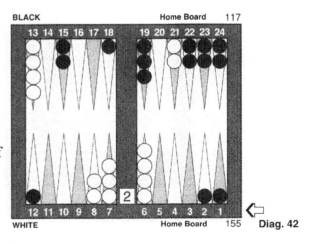

Diag. 42

The general rules for redoubling against a failed blitz are:

a) We must have made an anchor; without one the blitz may flare up again like a rash.

b) We generally need to have a solid four-prime with at least two checkers caught behind it. If we have trapped only one checker, it is too likely to escape into a winning race.

c) We need threats that will make the position a pass if we execute them, although we can redouble without threats if the position is already a pass.

Too Good

A blitz is often triggered off by a double which puts one or more checkers on the bar. When the opponent remains on the bar, use of the cube comes into consideration. Sometimes the opponent will dance with two checkers and we can consider playing on for an undoubled gammon:

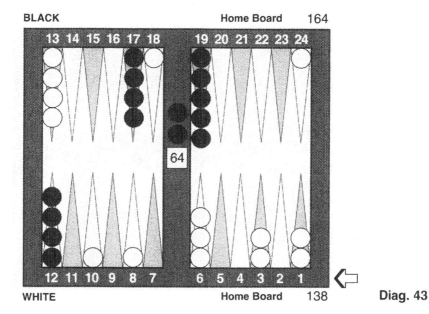

Diag. 43

This is a borderline position, after an opening 6-3 for White, played 24/18 13/10, a 5-2 in reply for Black, splitting to the 22-point and bringing a checker down with 13/8, followed by White's blitzing 5-5 and a dance. White has made a huge gain on the last roll, and in a money game has no alternative but to cash because of the Jacoby rule. In match play, however, even early in a match, it may be a marginal decision whether to play on for an undoubled gammon. The rollouts suggest that taking at least one more roll is correct:

BG	G	W	L	G	BG	CEq
1.4%	44.1%	73.4%	26.6%	5.1%	0.2%	1.02

Although the cubeless equity is only 0.87, which suggests a cash, White is very likely to offer a powerful double later, elevating the equity to 1.02 with the cube centred. Playing on runs the risk of Black's anchoring by rolling one of her three 'joker' doubles, but the risks are just about worth it.

A small change to the position makes it a clear error to play on, losing 0.04. The checker on White's 11-point is a less active builder. Also, White may not get an advanced anchor if Black does roll a joker.

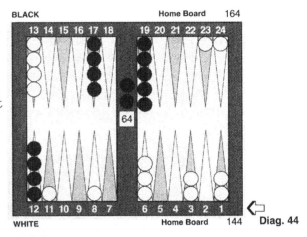

Diag. 44

Sometimes the player being blitzed can try for a gammon after rolling a joker. Here White has just entered with 5-5, hitting two checkers, and Black danced on the two-point board. Most players would play on, but the

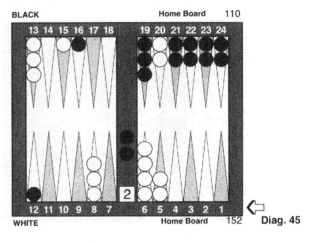

Diag. 45

rollouts show that this decision is narrowly wrong, with an equity of 1.96, owning a 2-cube. There is a tendency to underestimate the dangers and to take a roll in such positions, as the author did when facing the position. If the cube were in the centre, we would have to cash because of the Jacoby rule.

Exercise 5: White, on roll, has a five-point board here. What is the correct cube action?

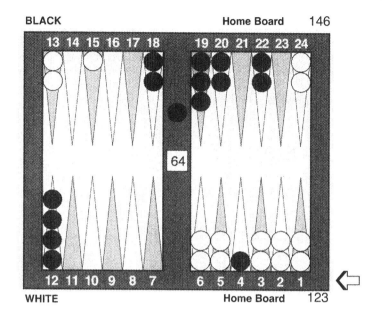

Diag. 46

Exercise 6: A 'bold or safe' decision in the next diagram. How should White play a 6-3? And how should he play at double match point?

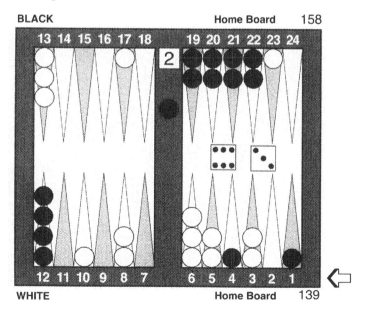

Diag. 47

Chapter Four

Calculating Equity

- **What is Equity?**
- **The 36-roll system**
- **Grouping Similar Rolls**
- **The Min-Max Method**

This chapter deals with the important subject of explaining and calculating the equity in a position. Modern computer programs use a numerical evaluation which shows the winning chances in a position and it is important to understand what this means and how it is derived.

What is Equity?

Equity in a money game means the value of a position. Before the dice have been rolled at the start of the game we have an equity of zero — we neither owe money nor have money owed to us. But with every roll of the dice and every cube turn until the end of the game this equity fluctuates. If we had to go man a lifeboat or catch a bus we might in principle end our game at any point by offering a settlement in which we pay — or get paid — whatever we can agree the equity to be at the time.

If there were no Jacoby Rule and we were certain to win a backgammon on an unturned cube our equity would be +3 and our opponent's would be –3. In the following position we can be equally precise; here we are certain to win a gammon; therefore our equity is +2 and our opponent's is –2.

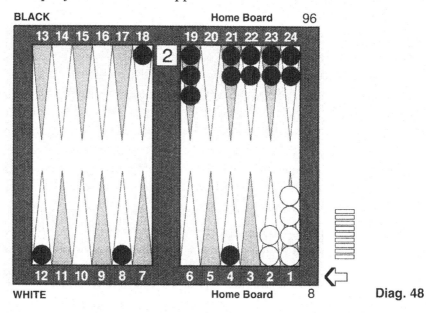

Diag. 48

Readers will notice that this definition of equity is cubeless. For the sake of simplicity it ignores the value of the cube (which is on 2, making our actual expectancy not +2 but +4).

And as we shall see cubeless equity (as the term suggests) ignores the drastic difference to the value of the position brought about when we factor in the power of the cube. There are three possibilities:

- The cube is centred.
- We own the cube.
- Our opponent owns the cube.

In our examples the certainty of the result of the game made the equity a simple, indisputable number. But what happens when all possible results are still on the cards — when both sides can still achieve plain wins, gammons and backgammons? In these cases we have to estimate equity by estimating the average number of points we think we will win and subtracting our estimate of the average number of points we think our opponent will win.

Note that equity in match play is more complex. We shall see in Part Two of this book that the terms of trade between our wins and losses of plain games, gammons and backgammons are usually quite different. They will differ at every match score and for every cube value. Moreover, in match play we can speak not only of the equity of positions but also of the equity of the scores themselves. Conventionally we express this value in percentage terms. If we're 0-0 in a match we clearly have equal chances to our opponent (the match length is irrelevant) and we can describe our match equity as 50%. If we achieve a lead of 1-0 in a 3-point match our equity is (we shall see shortly) around 60% — meaning that at the start of the next game we are 6 to 4 favourites to win the match. We shall see that we can derive fairly accurate equity figures for any scoreline and these figures are a vital part of the calculations and game plans of strong match players.

The 36-roll system

Working out the equity exactly in any position can be simple, as in our first example on the previous page, or very complicated. For example, when we are on roll after the opponent has rolled an opening 3-1 we are not able to work out the exact equity. Some positions, however, are conducive to a very accurate equity estimate:

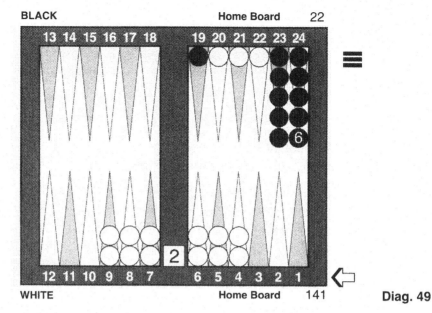

Diag. 49

Last Chance Saloon for White, who has 27 shots. If he hits, he will always win, because he owns the cube and Black will be unable to accept a redouble next turn. If White misses, Black will usually win a gammon, though not always, as White might roll enough doubles to get off it, or Black might roll 2-1 next and then get hit. Black will be on roll with 12 crossovers against 14 crossovers if White does not get a double. Working out gammon rates is often a bit tricky but we can get close if we know another table for when the crossovers are equal:

Crossovers	6 v 6	8 v 8	10 v 10	12 v 12
Gammon Rate	80%	75%	71%	68%

These are gammon rates for equal numbers of crossovers. In each case the trailer will be gammoned if he does not get a double. As we would expect, the more time the trailer has to get a double the more likely he is to get it. If the leader is a roll ahead, the trailer needs two doubles, and a good rule of thumb is to halve his chances in the above table. Let us estimate that Black wins 90% gammons and 10% single wins after White misses, ignoring the tiny chance of losing. This gives an equity of 1.8 + 0.1 = 1.9 per game over the nine misses. The equity can then be calculated as follows over 36 sample games:

27 x 1 for the hits = 27

9 x −1.9 for the misses = −17.1

This means that White is winning $(27 - 17.1) = 9.9$ points over 36 games and the equity is therefore $9.9/36 = 0.28$. As White owns a 2-cube we have to double this figure to give an equity of 0.56. The rollout results show that our estimates are close:

BG	G	W	L	G	BG	CEq
0.0%	0.0%	63.5%	36.5%	22.2%	0.2%	0.58

The cubeless equity is only 0.05, but the rollout with the cube in play resulted in an equity for White of 0.58 on a 2-cube.

We can also estimate the equity if we were Black and our opponent doubled us. 27 numbers would hit, but we would not now be certain to lose these. Our winning chances when we get closed out with three checkers off are approximately 15%. How do we know this? Well, we can use a rough-and-ready table:

Checkers Off	1	5	10	14
Winning Chances	5%	25%	75%	95%

Between one and five the winning chances go up in 5% jumps, as they do between 10 and 14. In the middle they go up in 10% jumps. This little chart is fairly accurate and has the virtue of being easy to remember. If the spares are perfectly placed, the player with the closed board will improve on these figures.

Of course, owning the cube we will do a bit better as well. As we advised earlier, a good rule is to add a sixth to our wins when we own the cube, so that we will win 17.5% of the time after we are hit. We thus win 17.5 and lose 82.5 out of 100 games for an equity of -0.65 $(.175 - .825)$ for each of the 27 hits. What about the misses? Well, we are clearly Too Good; our equity is almost identical to our earlier figure, 1.9.

We are now ready to combine the two figures:

27 x –0.65 for the hits

9 x 1.9 for the misses

Our overall equity is therefore $(27 \times -0.65 + 9 \times 1.9)/36 = (-0.35)/36 = -0.01$. This has to be multiplied by the new value of the cube, which will be 4, giving an equity of -0.04 for Black. So White is still a tiny favourite having given away the cube. This means that even though the double by White is hugely wrong (White has an equity of 0.58 owning a 2-cube), Black is not able to punish him with a beaver as her equity is negative.

For a correct double the cube-given-away equity needs to be greater than the cube-owned equity, taking into consideration the level of the cube in each case.

For a sound beaver the cube-owned equity needs to be greater than zero, although the cubeless equity may be negative.

Grouping Similar Rolls

It is impossible to analyse at the table more than 36 rolls for one side, although top computers usually analyse as many as 7776 variations, three moves ahead. We can, however, make a reasonable estimate of the equity for each of those 36 rolls, and a few errors may not be serious. Take the following position:

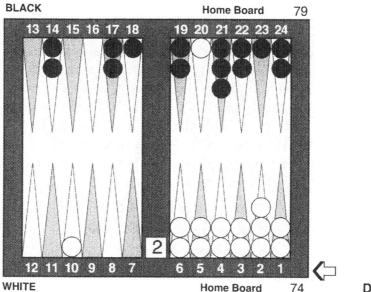

Diag. 50

White is on roll, leading in the race and with a winning shot. Several strong players thought this was a double/pass when I showed them the position. However, by breaking the next roll into four groups and estimating the equity for each, we can, within a few minutes, arrive at a fairly accurate estimate of the equity if Black takes a 2-cube.

a) The **11 hits** (all 2s) after which White is clearly Too Good and we will need to estimate a gammon rate.

b) The **12 rolls** (56, 55, 54, 53, 46, 44, 43) **which break contact** and become a race.

c) The **9 rolls** (combinations of 6s, 3s and 1s) **which stay put**.

d) The **4 rolls** (51, 41) **which partially escape**.

Let us estimate the equities, using the same processes employed by the author at the table :

a) After the **11 hits** White is Too Good and will win some gammons. How many? We can get a very good estimate of gammons when one or more checkers are closed out using the following method:

Count six crossovers for one checker closed out and an extra eight crossovers for any additional checkers closed out. Add the additional outfield crossovers, but count an extra $\frac{1}{2}$ crossover for any outfield crossover of four pips or more. Deduct five crossovers from the total and multiply the answer by 5%. Take away the number you first thought of … No, ignore that last instruction; the calculation is not as complicated as it seems. How does it work in our example? Well, after being hit, Black will have a checker on the bar (six crossovers) and four outfield crossovers plus one for having two crossovers of over four pips, a total of 11. We deduct five and multiply by 5% and get a gammon rate of 30%. This was confirmed by a rollout with a gammon rate of 32% after hitting. We can therefore assume an equity after hitting as follows:

> **30 gammons out of 100**
> **65 single wins out of 100**
> **5 losses out of 100**

This gives an equity of $(0.3 \times 2 + 0.65 - 0.05) = 1.2$. This was confirmed by a rollout after the average hit, 2-5, with an equity of 1.18. We do not need to make any adjustment for cube ownership as the cube is of little use to Black after being hit.

b) The **12 rolls that break contact** average 10 pips each, and put White 15 pips ahead in the race, but Black is on roll. Our formula on page 10 for the winning chances in a race can be modified for the player not on roll as follows:

$$P = 50\% + \frac{400L - R - 900}{R + 7L + 25} \%$$

R is the race length of the person on roll, L is the lead and P is the cubeless winning probability.

In our example L is 15 pips and our formula gives:

$$P = 50\% + (6000 - 79 - 900)/(79 + 105 + 25) = 24.4\%.$$

Again rollout results confirmed this estimate to be very accurate, with 25.5% race wins after we run with an average running roll of 6-4. We now need to adjust the equity for cube ownership. In a race we should add one sixth wins to our 24% to give us a cube-owned winning percentage of 28%. This gives a loss rate of 72% and thus an equity of about −0.4.

c) The **9 rolls that stay put** are hard to evaluate. No formula can help. In such cases ask yourself who you would rather be. If you cannot tell, use an evaluation of 0.0. If you prefer one side, ask if you would double for that side, assuming that player is on roll. If you are sure you wouldn't double, use an equity of +0.2 for the side you prefer. If you think you would double then use an equity of +0.4 for that side. If you think the position might be a borderline pass then use a cubeless equity of +0.6. If you know you would pass, and are not too good, use +0.8. If you do not know if you are too good use 1.00, etc. As you get more experienced you will be able to interpolate between these figures. Over the board, I did not know who was favourite after the stay-put numbers, although I suspected White was.

d) I was not sure either after the halfway house **rolls** 5-1 and 4-1 **which partially escape**, although here I thought Black probably was favourite, so I compromised and used an equity of zero for all 13 of the rolls in c) and d). However, zero is the cubeless figure, and we need to adjust for the value of the cube. To get a cube-owned equity we treat an equity of zero as 50% wins, and add one sixth more wins for owning the cube to give us a total of 58% wins. This means that we lose 42% and the equity on these 13 rolls, with the cube owned, works out to be +0.16 (0.58 − 0.42). Our three figures are therefore:

a) 11 hits at an equity of −1.2.

b) 12 races with an equity of −0.4.

c/d) 13 other numbers with an equity of +0.16.

The overall cube-owned equity therefore works out as:

$$(11 \times -1.2) + (12 \times -0.4) + (13 \times 0.16) = 15.92/36 = 0.44.$$

Our figures are based on a cube value of 1, so the equity on a 2-cube is −0.88, much better than passing, which will be −1.

A long rollout gave an equity of –0.83 after taking a 2-cube, even higher than our estimate. We cannot expect greater accuracy than this over the board in the time available. Potential sources of error will be the various formulas, which are only approximate, as well as small points we might miss such as White hitting with 2-1, say, but then crashing with 4-4, or White hitting with, say, 2-3, but then blotting with 6-6.

The Min-Max Method

In complicated positions we might have no idea what the equity is in certain variations, but we can adopt another approach. We find the main winning variation, estimate both its chance of occurring and its equity, and adjust upwards from there.

In principle, to accept a cube in a money game we need about 22% wins, but we have to add to this 1% for each 2% gammon losses that we sustain. If a main variation gives us around 20% wins, we do not need much from the subsidiary lines.

Take the following position:

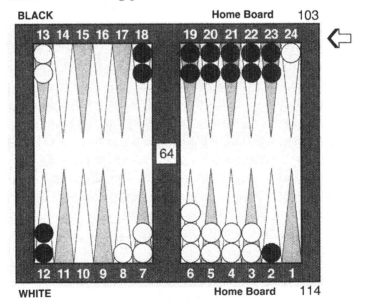

Diag. 51

In the early stages of a match, I doubled as Black here and my opponent passed immediately. 'Even if you miss I still have to cover to get an equal position,' he commented knowingly. This was an inaccurate simplification of the essential features of the position, which is an easy take and only a narrow double.

How should we tackle the position? Well, much as my opponent did, but with a different conclusion.

a) Black does not roll a six and White covers with a five. This occurs $^{25}/_{36}$ x $^{15}/_{36}$, which is around 30% of the time. White is a clear favourite in these lines, as he is level in the timing battle and owns the cube.

b) Black does not roll a six and White does not roll a five. Who knows what is happening? But Black still has to get over the five-prime, and may crash before she does.

c) Black rolls a six and White anchors with an ace. A clear pass, but an ace-point game offers around 15% wins, although it gets gammoned about the same amount of the time as well.

d) Black rolls a six and White does not get an ace. Very poor. These variations are clearly too good for Black.

We could, however, have stopped at a) above. If a variation which occurs as often as 30% of the time makes us a favourite, we do not need to get much from the other lines. Variation a) offers around 18% total wins and variation b), which occurs around 40% of the time, must offer about another 12% wins at least. Add in something for the ace-point game and we are getting around 35% wins, which even allowing for the gammons [mainly from (d)] makes the position an easy take, as the rollouts confirm:

BG	G	W	L	G	BG	Eq
1.0%	23.3%	65.0%	35.0%	4.1%	0.3%	0.69

The final figure is the equity from Black's point of view with White owning a 2-cube. So passing this position is a massive blunder, and the double is correct only because of the extreme volatility, with so much hinging on whether Black pops a six.

Sometimes it is the favourable variations that are difficult to analyse, while the unfavourable ones are pretty clear. In such cases we can adopt a different approach by calculating the equity and frequency of the clear lines. We then work out what equity we would need to have in the unclear lines for the position to be a take. We can often conclude that such an expectation is unrealistic, and this may well assist us in reaching a cube decision.

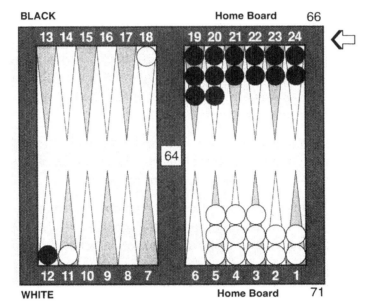

Diag. 52

Black leads by five pips in the race and has 17 winning shots. However, White will sometimes get a shot himself. We might not get the equity exactly right, but we can proceed as follows:

a) On the 16 hits other than 6-6, Black is winning a single game nearly all the time with a sprinkling of losses and gammons wins. Let us estimate these variations as having an equity of –2.00 if White accepts a 2-cube. The cube is of no great value to White in these lines.

b) The 10 rolls that get past and do not contain a six (5-5, 5-4, 5-3, 5-2, 4-4 and 4-3) average approximately 9 pips. White is then on roll, trailing 71-57, but with three extra crossovers. We adjust the pip count by adding one extra pip for each additional crossover, giving a revised pip-count of 74-57. We can again use our formula to calculate the winning chances for the player not on roll:

$$P = 50\% + \frac{400L - R - 900}{R + 7L + 25}\%$$

This gives winning chances for our opponent of:

$$50 + (6800 - 74 - 900)/(74 + 119 + 25) = 77\%.$$

Thus White has around 23% wins and we can add one sixth — 4% — for cube ownership, giving White 27% wins and an equity of –0.46 (0.27 – 0.73), or –0.92 on a 2-cube.

On the 16 hits, therefore, after accepting a 2-cube, White will lose 32 points, and after the 10 'scoot-past' rolls he will lose 9.2 points.

c) In order to do better than he achieves by passing, White will need to lose a total of no more than 36 points in 36 games. As he is already losing 41.2 points in variations (a) and (b) he needs to win a net 5.2 points in the 10 games in which Black cannot get past and offers a shot (including the rogue 6-6 which blots). This requires an equity of +0.52 per game. White has only a single shot, which is not certain to win, and is otherwise around 9 pips down in the race, so it is very hard to decide who is favourite. White will gain from holding the cube, but an equity of +0.52 is clearly too optimistic, and the position is a clear pass. The rollouts after Black's 3-1, played 13/9, and shown in diagram 53, confirmed this, with White a 49-51 underdog, although, owning a 2-cube, he has a positive equity of +0.28.

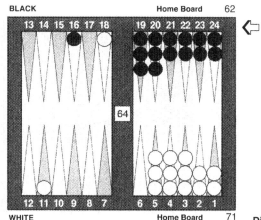

Diag. 53

The overall rollouts also confirmed the pass:

BG	G	W	L	G	BG	CEq
0.0%	3.7%	78.6%	21.4%	0.2%	0.0%	1.11

The final figure is the equity for Black having cubed. It is much greater than one, so it is a blunder for White to accept the cube.

Calculating equity in unusual positions is more difficult again. One good approach is to ask yourself two questions:

a) What is the worst type of position I can get?

b) What is the best type of position I can get?

If the worst scenario is several checkers closed out, it is no good hoping that you can get into a deuce-point game; this will go nowhere near to compensating you for the gammon losses.

Exercise 7: Black has just entered from the bar with 4-2 and played the excellent b/21 5/3* — the so-called 'banana split', which breaks two points in one's own board to hit an opposing checker as a tempo play. Try to work out White's equity with the cube owned and the equity if Black takes a redouble.

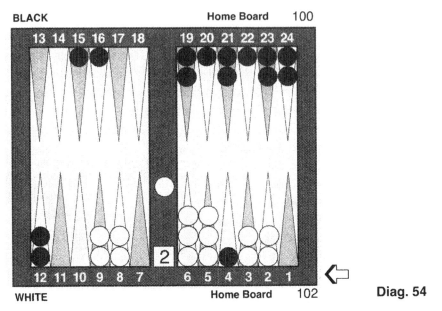

Diag. 54

Exercise 8: A crushed position this time. Estimate the equity again with White owning the cube, and also if Black takes a redouble. You should then know the correct cube action.

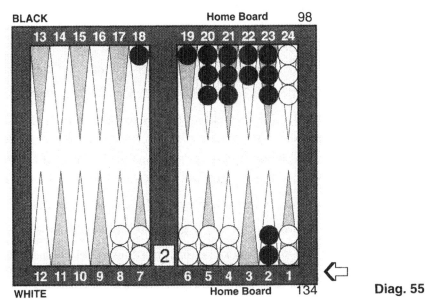

Diag. 55

Exercise 9: A volatile position in which White's next roll is critical. Estimate the equity for the hits, dances and other entry numbers, and again you should know the cube decision.

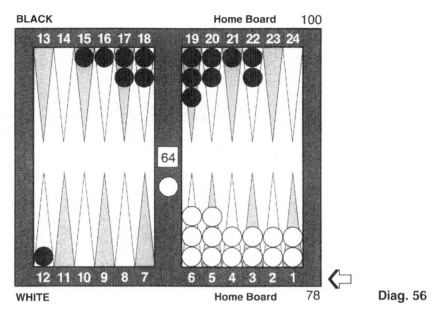

Diag. 56

Exercise 10: Again the next roll for White is important, but this time he may get further bites at the cherry. Working out the equity is quite tough here.

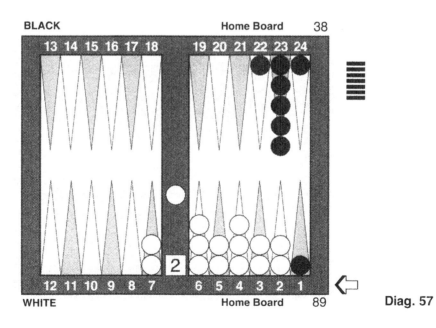

Diag. 57

Part Two

Mastering Match Play

---

by Simon Gasquoine

and Paul Lamford

Chapter Five

The Basics

■ **Introduction**

■ **Practical Considerations**

■ **The Match Equity Chart**

■ **A Match-Equity Formula**

■ **Risk-Reward Ratios**

Doubling Points
Take points
Windows

■ **GReW**

■ **Two Targets**

Introduction

Can you work out the correct cube actions here, for money and at the scores indicated in the diagrams?

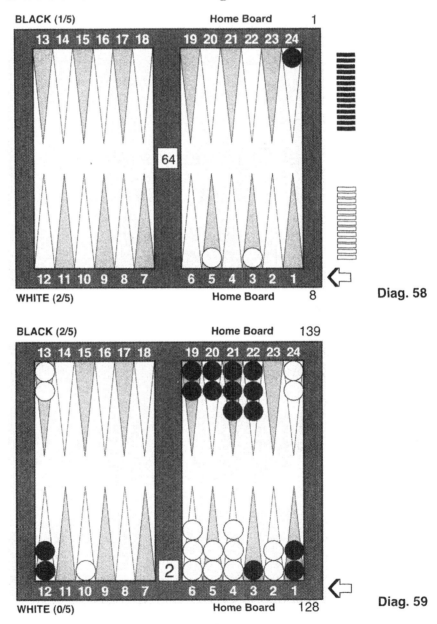

Diag. 58

Diag. 59

If you said that they are no double/beavers for money but double/takes at the scores: well done indeed. If not: welcome to the demanding world of match backgammon!

Match play and money play are very different games — and there is no doubt that it is match play which poses the tougher challenges. Not the least of these arises because backgammon tournaments — unlike, for example, their chess or golf equivalents — are so democratic. Not many of us will be going the distance with Gary Kasparov or teeing off with Tiger Woods any day soon. But backgammon competitions are normally unseeded events, open to allcomers. If you're prepared to stump up the Open Division entry fee, you may find yourself up against a living legend in the opening round.

That's an exciting prospect. But the winning chances of the average player facing (say) the World Champion would be far greater if they were to meet instead in the late-night chouette in the bar. In match play the familiar fixed odds of money play become fluid, and making the right decisions is a lot more complicated. This gives the expert player a big advantage, and can make money backgammon seem by comparison as frivolously easy as noughts and crosses.

Practical Considerations

The complexities of match backgammon are endlessly fascinating but they can provoke defeatism in even the boldest and most clued-up of money players. How can ordinary mortals hope to solve the conundrums of match backgammon at the table? After all, match-play rules deny us the benefits of pen and paper, let alone calculators and equity charts. Opponents can also become irritated by excessive pause for thought.

Of course we mustn't be put off by these pressures. But time constraints may limit our ability to calculate. Although backgammon lags behind chess in the extent and sophistication with which time controls are imposed on players, clocks are increasingly used in major tournaments (old-fashioned chess clocks, unfortunately, not the Fischer clocks much better suited to the game). This also applies when we play on the internet. Tight limits on thinking time are imposed on servers such as the excellent truemoneygames.com.

What's more, when we play on the internet a further delicate question arises: the opponent's fear that we might not be playing entirely ethically. Significant delays over decisions are prone to arouse grave suspicions. Are we are phoning a friend? Possibly not; but could it be that we are frantically seeking guidance from our analytic software — Snowie, Jellyfish or one of the many good free programs which we can download from the internet?

So we often have to make compromises over the board — mental short-cuts on the way to victory. All the same, any halfway-serious match player needs to know his way round the match equity chart, understand how it can be used to make vital decisions and be prepared — when the occasion demands — to crunch some numbers at the board.

The Match Equity Chart

What are your chances of winning a backgammon match which has reached, say, 10-9 to you when the first person to reach 11 is the winner? Questions such as this occur regularly in your calculations towards the end of a close match, and the correct decisions which depend on the answer are likely to vary considerably from those which would be right in a money game.

What we need to answer this sort of question is a match equity chart: a table showing our percentage chances of winning the match from all possible scores. This is a far more complex question than, for instance, computing the chances of snooker players winning their matches from different scores, because in a backgammon match the score doesn't necessarily move in simple increments of one point. Backgammon players eight points adrift of the winning post may win the match in one fell swoop with a 4-cube gammon; snooker players have to grind out eight wins. And just to complicate matters further, in backgammon there's the Crawford game.

During the 1980s a number of leading American authorities on the game (including Danny Kleinman, Bill Robertie and Roy Friedman) published equity tables. These varied surprisingly widely, mainly because of the different gammon rates assumed. The table which is used by most players today is the work of another U.S. expert, Kit Woolsey, and can be found in his short book *How to Play Tournament Backgammon*, published in 1993. Woolsey derived his chart from a combination of maths and empirical data — a huge database of matches compiled by top Canadian player, Hal Heinrich.

But a more recent chart, the work of one of the present authors, is used here and given opposite. Calculated from first principles by Lamford, this chart nevertheless agrees closely at

Match Equity Chart for an 11-point match based on a gammon rate of 25%

	1PC	1CR	2	3	4	5	6	7	8	9	10	11
1PC	50	—	51	69	70	82	83	89	90	94	94	96
1CR	—	—	69	75	82	85	89	91	94	95	96	97
2	49	31	50	60	67	74	80	84	87	90	92	94
3	31	25	40	50	57	65	71	76	80	84	87	89
4	30	18	33	43	50	58	64	70	74	78	82	85
5	18	15	26	35	42	50	57	62	67	72	76	80
6	17	11	20	29	36	43	50	56	61	66	71	75
7	11	9	16	24	30	38	44	50	55	61	65	69
8	10	6	13	20	26	33	39	45	50	55	60	65
9	6	5	10	16	22	28	34	39	45	50	55	59
10	6	4	8	13	18	24	29	35	40	45	50	55
11	4	3	6	11	15	20	25	31	35	41	45	50

PC = Post Crawford   CR = Crawford   Numbers in bold are points needed to win most scores with that of Woolsey and, more recently, the equity figures generated by the computer program Snowie.

The bold figures in the chart down the left side and along the top indicate the number of points required by each side to win the match. For instance, a score of 8-6 in an 11-point match is expressed as 3 away/5 away and the chart gives the leader's match-winning chances of 65%. It would be possible to generate a chart for longer matches but the 11-point chart will be quite sufficient for our purposes in these chapters. Even in matches of greater length it is usually the scores nearest to the finish that generate the most critical equity-based decisions.

How is the chart generated? Well, returning to the question in the first paragraph on this page, if you are 10-9 ahead in an 11-point match, it first depends on whether the next game is the Crawford game. If it is **not the Crawford game** (that is to say, it is 'Post-Crawford'), your opponent may well double immediately and the match will be on the line. Your chances of winning the match are about 50%. In fact, for a reason we'll discuss later on, the 'free pass', they are actually around 51%. This is shown by the figure 51% for PC (i.e. Post-Crawford) 1 v 2 in the chart.

If the next game **is the Crawford game**, your opponent needs to win two games or one game in which she achieves a gammon. How often is a gammon won? Surveys of world-class matches and rollouts of the starting position by Snowie suggest a frequency of around 25%.

This means the opponent will achieve 100% match equity $1/8$ of the time (by immediately winning a gammon) — which equates to 12.5% match equity. $3/8$ of the time she achieves 50% match equity tied at DMP (double match point). $3/8$ of 50% is 18.75% Add the two percentages together and we find the total match winning chances (and therefore our take point): 31.25%. Accordingly in the table, for 2 v 1CR (Crawford), we find the rounded value 31.

Of course, not all equities are as easy to establish as this one. But the principle is always the same: the match equity chart is compiled by working from simple scores like this one outwards to more complex ones. The calculations soon become immensely complicated by the need to factor in the effects of all possible recubes by both players. And we will only touch upon the complicated match equity calculations that take into consideration the difference in skill of the players.

A Match Equity Formula

Before we move on to look at the way the chart is used, we need to decide to **learn** it (or as much of it as we can) or else know a way to **reconstruct** it.

However, there is no need to know the Post-Crawford scores at all; they are there for information and do not affect cube decisions. Post-Crawford cube action is relatively simple (although there are a few tricks which we will look at later).

A decent match player should learn the **Crawford scores**, however — the third row and the third column of the table. The easiest way to do this is to learn the sequence from the trailer's point of view:

3   4   5   6   9   11   15   18   25   31

These numbers show the percentage winning chances when trailing Crawford game, from 11 away/1 away to 2 away/1 away. Note that we always learn two values for the price of one. Once we've worked out that the trailer has 3% match equity trailing Crawford game 11-away/1 away, we also know the leader must have $(100 - 3)\% = 97\%$.

It is also well worth learning the equities for scores where either player is **2 points from victory**, because no formula can reconstruct these accurately enough.

However, we have a choice of methods of approximating the remainder of the values at the table and of working out values for longer matches when we need to know them. Curiously, Lamford and a colleague, Rick Janowski, simultaneously developed two slightly different but essentially similar formulas for this purpose. Rick's is the one often quoted in backgammon literature, so we shall attempt to redress the balance by giving Lamford's equation:

$$\mathbf{P} \quad = \quad 50\% \quad + \quad \frac{5L}{6T + 36}\ \%$$

where P is the match-winning percentage, L is the lead in points and T is the number of points required by the trailer.

Let's see how this is calculated in practice. For an example we'll consider the score 5-3 in an 11-point match. Our lead is 2 points (i.e. 5 minus 3) and the number of points required by the trailer is 8 (i.e. 11 minus 3). Plugging these figures into our formula gives the equation:

$$P = 50\% + (10)/(48 + 36) = 62\%$$

The chart gives 61%; the formula is usually accurate to within 1%.

Risk-Reward Ratios

Why do we need to know the chances of winning a match at a given score? It is because whenever you offer or accept a cube in a match you need to know what odds you are getting on your action. You would be crazy to place a complicated football spread bet without working out your maximum possible gain (the reward) and loss (the risk). Exactly the same applies to playing backgammon matches. The point of match equities is that they enable us to calculate the relevant risk-reward ratios.

Let us start off with a simple position, which all readers of this book should be able to work out to be a redouble/take in a money game:

No excuse for failing to count winning and losing rolls in these sorts of positions. Here White wins immediately with 6-6, 5-5, 4-4, 3-3, 2-2, 6-5, 6-4, 6-3, 6-2, 5-4, 5-3 and 5-2 — a total of 19 rolls, making him a slight money favourite, about

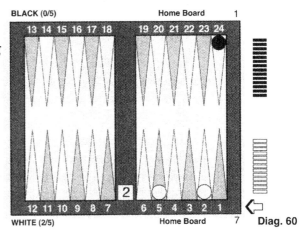

BLACK (0/5)　　　　　Home Board　　1

WHITE (2/5)　　　　　Home Board　　7　Diag. 60

53% (19/36) to win. This small edge wouldn't usually justify a money double (in fact it would normally prompt a correct beaver!). But White won't get another chance to use the cube and Black never gets a chance to return it. Therefore it is correct to double or redouble for money. Of course, Black's take is trivial.

The doubling point

But what is right for money may be utterly wrong in a match. Here White, owning a 2-cube, is 3 away/5 away. (You should familiarise yourself with the need to think all the time about scores in terms of the number of points each side has to go; not to think 'I'm trailing 13-14 in a 17-point match … eek! Uncharted territory!', but rather 'I'm 4 away/3 away … No sweat! Familiar situation'.)

To work out White's doubling point we have to know the match equity of the different possible outcomes. First let's compare the equities when White wins, with and without the recube.

a) White doubles and wins to win the match — match equity **100%**.

b) White does not double and wins to lead 1 away/5 away, match equity **85%**.

So the recube could gain a **reward** of (100 – 85) = **15%**.

In the same way, now we compare the equities when White loses, once again with and without the recube:

c) White doubles and loses the game, match equity at 3 away/ 1 away of **25%**.

d) White does not double and loses to tie at 3 away/3 away, equity **50%**.

So the recube runs a **risk** of (50 – 25) = **25%**.

Note that the issue is not complicated here by the possibility of either side using the cube later. This will be the last roll of the game. Note also that two of these figures — the equity if we double and win (100%) and the equity if we don't double and lose (50%) — shouldn't require anyone to toil with the Lamford formula!

Now we know the risk and the reward a simple formula gives us the doubling point:

$$\textbf{Doubling Point} \ = \ \frac{\textbf{Risk}}{\textbf{Risk + Reward}}$$

Inserting the values we have worked out gives this equation:

Doubling point = 25/(15 + 25) = **62.5%**.

The take point

Working out the doubling point involved knowing four equities; working out the take point is slightly easier as we only need to know three:

a) Black can pass to trail 1 away/5 away Crawford with a match equity of **15%**.

b) She can take and win the game to lead 1 away/3 away Crawford — match equity **75%**.

c) Black can take and lose with match equity of **0%**.

So the take nets a **reward** of (75 –15) = **60%** when Black wins but runs a risk of (15 – 0) = **15%** when it loses.

We use the same formula to compute the take point that we used to find the doubling point:

$$\text{Take Point} \quad = \quad \frac{\text{Risk}}{\text{Risk} + \text{Reward}}$$

Once again, inserting the values we have worked out gives this calculation:

Take point = 15/(15 + 60) = **20%**

The doubling window

Taken together, the doubling point and the take point give us the two ends of what we term the doubling window. The doubler needs to work out the doubling point; the player being doubled needs to work out the take point. When we give doubling windows we express the take point from the doubler's point of view — here, not as 20%, but as 80% (i.e. 100-20%). From the doubler's point of view, this is the cashpoint, beyond which the opponent never has a correct take. In our example, we are only winning 53% of the time so we are not in the window. Unlike for money, the position is **No Double/Take**.

Note also that we should be perfectly content to work with rounded figures. It is quite good enough to describe the window as 63% to 80%. Rounding may introduce a small element of inaccuracy into our calculations, but it will seldom lose us much equity. In most positions there will be far more inaccuracy in our estimates of winning chances and gammons.

GReW

If only we could always base our decisions on these neat, exact calculations! The position we have been discussing is susceptible to precise calculation. We could work out exactly what the winning chances were and could be equally precise about the doubling window. But it is more common for doubles to be made in complex early or middle-game positions.

The acronym GREW reminds us of the three crucial complications:

■   **Gammons**

■   **Redoubles**

■   **Wastage**

The last of these, wastage, means that a player cannot use all the points available. In Diagram 60 on page 66 above, we've seen our first example of this: only Black can use all four points available after a redouble/take. This is one of the features which makes this position not a double.

Two Targets

As backgammon matches come to the crunch, gammon wins and losses become much more important than in money play. In matches we should always be looking to maximise the value of our own gammons and to minimise the value of our opponent's. And if we are getting full value for our gammons — meaning there is no wastage — they will usually be worth more than for money, sometimes even twice as much. (The precise amounts are presented in the Gammon Values Chart on page 101.)

This is because gammons are the fast track to two desirable goals: getting to the Crawford game, where we are protected from our opponent's cube; or, better still, the winner's enclosure, where we can gloat in triumph. We should aim whenever possible for the scores and the cubes which can propel us, in a single game, to one or other of these destinations — and we should be remembering that our opponent is (or should be) thinking along these lines too.

The desirability of getting straight to the winning post isn't too hard to see. It isn't rocket science to grasp that when you are two points from home an undoubled gammon fills the bill perfectly; or that if your opponent needs four points you want an advanced anchor to minimise her gammons and thereby avert the unpleasant offer of an early cube. However, the desirability of getting to the Crawford game tends to be underrated by players. For example, beginners are often told, quite wrongly, that the score 0-0 in a 5-point match

(5 away/5 away) can be played more or less like a money game. This is poor advice. Consider Diagram 61 in which the roller has a powerful blitz:

The double is clear both for money and at the score. But it is a significant error either to pass for money or to take at this score. The explanation of the difference is that in the match situation the leader's doubled gammons are worth more than

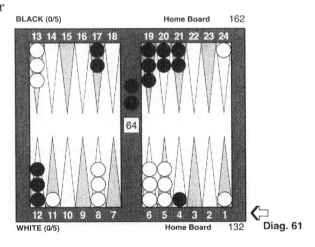

Diag. 61

for money because they get him straight to the Crawford game.

The equities are –0.92 having accepted a 2-cube for money, and the equivalent of –1.05 after taking at this score. The latter figure incorporates an adjustment for the value of gammons.

It is an even more expensive mistake to treat a 3 away/3 away game like a money game, as Diagram 62 shows.

This is a clear money take but a huge pass at the score. Why? In this almost gammonless position, Black gets to the Crawford game with a doubled plain win. White must pass and look for an early cube, preferably

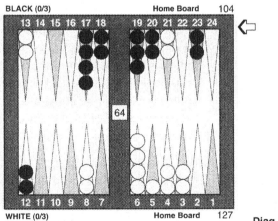

Diag. 62

with a gammon threat, in the next game.

The equities are –0.95 for money and –1.21 at the score, again a significant difference, and this time in a quiet non-gammonish position.

Exercise 11: Work out the take points in a race at the following scores:

a) 3 away/3 away; initial cube.

b) 3 away/3 away; recube.

c) 4 away/5 away; initial cube.

d) 11 away/3 away; recube.

Exercise 12: Work out if you would double and whether you would take in the diagram below at each of the following scores:

a) 3 away/4 away.

b) 4 away/3 away.

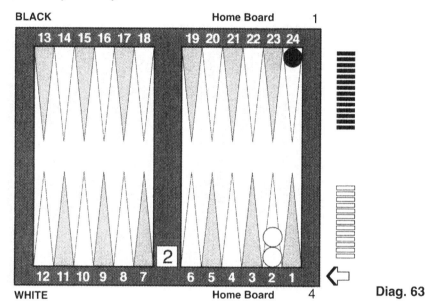

Diag. 63

Exercise 13: Change the above diagram to give White a 4-cube on his side. Again decide the cube action for both sides at each of the following scores:

a) 5 away/5 away.

b) 5away/8 away.

c) 8 away/8 away.

Chapter Six

Special Scores

- **Double Match Point**
- **2 Away/2 Away**
- **The Crawford Game**
- **Post-Crawford Scores**

Double Match Point

We start with what might seem to be the simplest of scorelines. No complexities here, surely? The game is of course cubeless, so that eliminates a great swathe of possible errors for a start. All we have to do is win! Gammons and backgammons no longer count. But this simplification creates a form of backgammon to which we're otherwise unaccustomed. There's the rub.

The term DMP shouldn't be restricted to that final match game in which each side is a single point from victory. Once the score and cube value determine that the present game must be the last of the match (0-0 in a 7-point match with the cube on 8, say), we have effectively reached DMP.

What can we say in general terms about checker play at DMP? Those checker plays and overall game plans which involve taking the extra risks justified when gammons count should be downgraded. Wimpy running plays rate higher than normal. Gonzo blitzes rate lower. Slotting with an opening 2-1 and 5-1 beats splitting. But it isn't so easy to establish a neat set of general rules. For instance: advanced anchors no longer ward off gammons, but though the ace-point, we are always told, 'keeps us in the game until the end', making the golden anchor may actually give us the more flexible game.

To take just one example of these perplexities: what is the DMP play here?

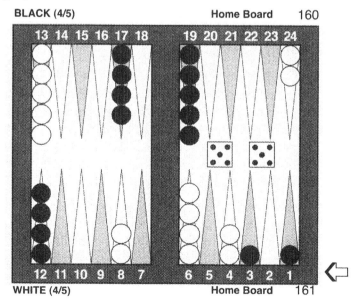

Diag. 64

For money there's nothing to think about: the double whammy 8/3*(2) 6/1*(2) is best by the length of the street. At DMP, however, the more positional 13/3*(2) might be played by those aware that gammons are of no value at this score; but the all-out blitz play is still best (although by a far shorter distance), as it is simply the best way to win the game. There are many examples of DMP decisions throughout the book.

Remember that the DMP game is the most important game of the match. Why? Because both players have all their match equity on the line. We may play abominably in the nervous opening game of our 25-point World Championship final match, but without fatal consequences — unless the cube changes hands several times, the amount of match equity we are liable to lose is a single figure percentage, probably a low one at that. But at DMP the equity loss incurred by every little error is hugely magnified. It is therefore vital at this (and other late scores) to be prepared to slow down and play the most accurate backgammon we can muster.

2 away/2 away

No prizes for knowing the doubling point at this score. Whenever both sides need the same number of points, the doubling point is clearly 50%.

What about the take point? After a double/take we are effectively playing for the match at DMP; our take point is therefore our winning chance if we were instead to pass and trail Crawford 2 away/1 away, which we calculated above to be worth about 31%.

The orthodoxy propounded by most backgammon literature today is that the game should always finish with the cube on 2. If one player doesn't double, the other one will — and if both players can contrive not to lose their markets by pointlessly waiting too long, their cubes should always be taken. The logical conclusion reached is that there's really nothing to be lost at 2 away/2 away from doubling at the first legal opportunity.

But readers who've played any amount of match backgammon should smell a rat here. This reasoning would be fine if we could assume perfect knowledge and cube handling by our opponents. But in fact we have here to consider the complicating effects of skill difference on match decisions. Even if our opponents do know the take point here, an immediate double on our part still deprives them (and, admittedly, us too!) of the opportunity to make a cube error.

And suppose our opponents don't know the take point? Now if the game goes against us, we're gaining big time if the cube has stayed in the centre. We can hope to get an extended 'free ride' during which we may manage to turn the game around whilst our opponents close in on what they may very likely be unable to distinguish from a normal money cube. Unless they get really lucky and play on successfully for an undoubled gammon, we can expect them to overshoot the far end of the doubling window in the process and wind up doubling us not in but out, leaving us still alive, gratefully clinging on to our 2 away/1 away 31% match equity. And having established their misconceptions about the take point, if we can turn the game around, we can delay our own double, knowing that they will (if they're consistent) be taking too late.

Of course our opponents may know all this. They may well be thinking: what does he know about this scoreline? Does he know how high the take point is? A sudden reversal of fortune (a blitz 5-5 followed by a dance), and one player may wind up playing for an undoubled match-winning gammon.

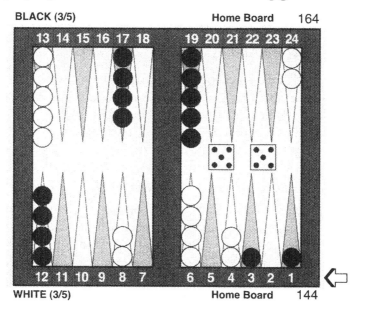

Diag. 65

For example, the position above occurred after Black danced on her second move — the Poirots among you will have no difficulty reconstructing the game. White correctly didn't double before his last roll, and it is now right for him to play on (rather than cash the game — Black should pass if doubled) as his gammon wins comfortably exceed his losses. This position shows that the theorists are not even right in theory!

So, of all scorelines, this is the one where received theory and good practice should diverge most drastically. The conventional advice must be stood on its head: never double at the first opportunity at this score. When you are 2 away/2 away, knowing what your opponents know and what they think you know are invaluable. So get second-guessing!

The Crawford Game

The leader can obviously never win a gammon or backgammon that counts, but the trailer can.

There are essentially two types of Crawford game:

(a) Those in which the trailer needs an **even** number of points to win the match; so the trailer should aggressively go for the gammon if possible and it is the leader's task to prevent this.

(b) Those in which he needs an **odd** number, and gammons therefore only count for the value of the free pass — as explained below. Note, though, that backgammons could come in very handy! So avoid ace-point games at Crawford 1 away/3 away: they raise the backgammon rate and could take your opponent straight to the winning post.

Post-Crawford Scores

After the Crawford game, the trailer will surely always want to double — after all, he has nothing to lose. But when should he double? Immediately? If not, why not? How does the leader decide whether to take or pass? And will the trailer ever correctly abstain from doubling altogether?

Once again, we make a fundamental distinction between scores at which the trailer needs an even number of points and those at which he needs an odd number.

Let's examine each of these in turn.

(a) The trailer needs an even number of points

At these scores the leader is said to have a **free pass** of the cube. Whether he takes or passes is a fairly minor decision, Take for instance the score Crawford 4 away/1 away. The trailer needs two doubled single wins or one doubled gammon to win the match. But exactly the same will apply to the following game if the leader exercises his free pass. In other words, the scores Post-Crawford 4 away/1 away and Post-Crawford 3 away/1 away differ only in the availability of the free pass itself — worth approximately 1% of match equity — and in the fact that from 3 away, backgammons win the match.

When the leader wins the opening roll, any roll except 4-1 or 2-1 gives him a correct take of the trailer's cube. How do we figure this out? Winning the opening roll is an advantage in itself. The leader should therefore take as he is a slight favourite. The two exceptions are the particularly uninspiring rolls of 4-1 and 2-1, which make him a slight underdog and therefore give him a pass. Some players reason this wrongly. They ask why, if they fail to get a really good opening roll — 3-1, 4-2, 6-5, 6-1 or 5-3 would all do nicely — should they not pass and have another go? The fallacy of this argument is surely obvious — the opponent is equally likely to get the good number next time.

When the trailer wins the opening roll, he should avoid slotting plays because he can never benefit from them. If the leader hits, not only has the slot failed but it has made the take clear; if he misses, the slot has achieved nothing for the trailer because the leader should now automatically pass the cube.

What about gammon threats? Recently some leading players have discovered that the trailer may actually withhold the cube if the opening sequence generates an immediate gammon threat. After an opening 3-1 and a poor reply (4-1 or 2-1), the leader will clearly pass if the cube is turned. Therefore the trailer should play on for as long as the possibility of an undoubled gammon overshadows the possibility of becoming an underdog before the next opportunity to turn the cube. However, this is a dangerous way for the intermediate player to pursue an advantage which may well never materialise. It shouldn't be attempted unless you know exactly what you are doing. (Be prepared to lose face, by the way: most opponents and kibitzers will assume you have simply forgotten to double.)

Note that the leader only gets **one** free pass, because after he has exercised it the trailer is henceforth pursuing an even number of points. So if the trailer is miles behind, needing to win a long sequence of games, it makes sense for the leader to withhold the free pass until he gets a really disadvantageous opening sequence.

(b) The trailer needs an odd number of points

These scores, conversely, give the leader a mandatory take because a pass would bring the trailer a whole game nearer to victory. So when should the trailer double? Readers who've played any amount of match backgammon will have observed that only the most ignorant, absent-minded or intoxicated opponents fail to double immediately.

But are they right to do so? In a parallel universe, populated by really classy backgammon players who never miscalculate anything, there would be no reason for delay. But, in this world, the immediate cube turn is wrong. Delay! The leader should be taking in a game with few or no gammons if he has even the tiniest smidgen of a chance of winning, so there's nothing at all to be lost from waiting. (Except your reputation: once again, opponents will assume amnesia has struck you — though Snowie will be nodding approvingly at your strategy). Now things may get very interesting indeed if you manage to generate some sort of evident gammon threat. A cube offer now could scoop a huge match equity gain.

This position arose in a match on the internet server FIBS and the leader — who had up to this point probably been assuming White had forgotten to double — blundered horribly by passing the delayed cube. Now White is a whole

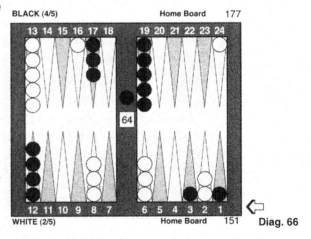

BLACK (4/5)　　　Home Board　177

64

WHITE (2/5)　　　Home Board　151　Diag. 66

game nearer the winning post. Opponents, used to making the mandatory take of an immediate cube, are prone to get wonderfully discombobulated by this tactic. Recognising that there's a gammon threat, they may panic and pass trivial takes.

Only when the chance of being gammoned **exceeds the winning chances** is a pass correct. So: never double immediately in this situation; wait until you can give your opponent the chance to blunder. Paul Magriel calls this ploy 'the trick'. But do not delay too long; you may lose your market.

Exercise 14: White trails 2 away/1 away Crawford. Should he bear off aggressively, volunteering a direct shot but generating more gammons, or should he play safe?

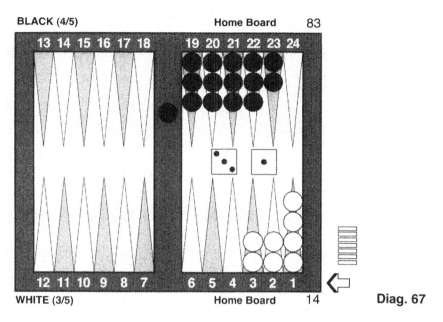

Exercise 15: A double match point problem. Do you make the golden anchor or the golden point?

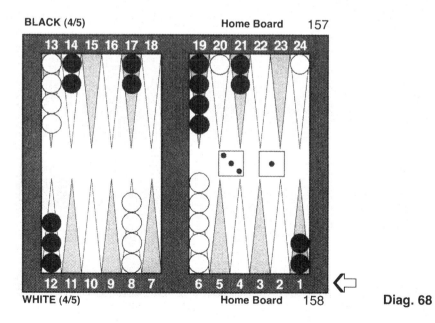

Chapter Seven

Doubling Windows

- **The Charts**
- **Doubling when you are two away**
- **Too Good but Not Good Enough**
- **Doubling when the opponent is two away**

In Chapter Six we introduced the concept of the doubling window: the range of percentage winning chances which is bounded at one end by the minimum theoretical doubling point and at the other by the last theoretically possible take point. We saw how we can work out windows when there are no redoubling possibilities to complicate the issue.

It is important to practise these kinds of risk-reward calculations until you are confident you can do them at the table. But certain windows will clearly crop up again and again, and readers should be prepared to learn as many of these as they can. We shall now present three charts of doubling windows: vital match play information which, as far as the authors are aware, is published in this form nowhere else in backgammon literature today.

The Charts

These charts are generated from the match equity table given in the previous chapter — but are broadly similar to those generated by computer programs such as Snowie. (We can access Snowie's version of these data at individual scores — though not in the form of a chart — in the program's Theory panel.) The figure in the top right of each cell is the doubling point; the figure in the bottom left is the cashpoint (the take point viewed from the doubler's point of view).

Explanation of the precise method of calculation of the windows would go far beyond the scope of this book. Readers who are tempted to try to verify these figures are cautioned that the programming required is complex, particularly as it involves the need to factor in recubes — and recubes of recubes!

But readers are more likely to be sceptical of the practical worth to be derived from studying windows at all. So much data! And isn't all this merely the tip of a vast and scary iceberg? When, it might be objected, do we ever find both ourselves and our opponents expecting to win 25% gammons — the situation assumed by Table Two below? Well, that's an easy one: as we explained on page 64, whenever we set up the checkers to start a backgammon game! That's one of the reasons that this particular table is so invaluable. Okay, but aren't we going to have to be forever generating new tables for all match lengths, all scores, all cube values, all gammon ratios; and to what purpose? Isn't this really just for armchair theorists, unhelpful to ordinary players in the cut-and-thrust of their matches? Anyway, doesn't this plethora of data break the promise made at the beginning of the chapter that practical guidance would be offered?

In fact, there's plenty of purpose to studying these tables. In a backgammon game we rely all the time on that which we have learnt in the past and which we don't therefore have to attempt to work out at the table. We can't be forever either guessing or trying to calculate over the board something as recurrently relevant as the 2 away/3 away gammonless window. The ambitious tournament player will memorise, at the very least, some of the most common, vital or surprising windows. Hard work for most of us, of course, but a source of huge advantage over all those players who are blundering in the dark.

■ Chart One gives the gammonless windows for all scores in an 9-point match (adequate for most purposes).

■ Chart Two gives the windows for 25% gammons. A comparison of Tables One and Two shows us how gammon windows shift in response to gammon threats.

■ Chart Three gives the windows for gammonless recubes.

In each chart, the person doubling or redoubling is A.

Chart 1: Gammonless Doubling Window

A Needs		1	2	3	4	5	6	7	8	9
					B Needs					
2	From	-	50	67	77	70	69	70	74	72
	To	-	69	75	82	78	79	79	82	81
3	From	-	57	50	38	40	43	46	42	45
	To	-	73	76	78	79	78	80	80	82
4	From	-	65	62	50	44	47	46	44	43
	To	-	81	81	81	80	79	78	79	79
5	From	-	68	60	56	50	52	50	48	48
	To	-	82	82	83	81	81	81	81	81
6	From	-	59	57	53	48	50	48	47	46
	To	-	78	79	80	79	79	79	79	79
7	From	-	60	54	54	50	52	50	49	48
	To	-	78	78	79	79	79	79	79	79
8	From	-	60	58	56	52	53	51	50	48
	To	-	80	80	80	80	79	79	79	79
9	From	-	60	55	57	52	54	52	52	50
	To	-	79	79	80	80	80	80	80	80

Chart 2: Doubling Windows for a Gammon Rate of 25%

A Needs		1	2	3	4	5	6	7	8	9
					B Needs					
2	From	-	50	71	81	78	81	84	88	86
	To	-	69	75	82	80	83	84	88	86
3	From	-	46	50	52	50	50	52	52	54
	To	-	65	71	74	77	78	81	83	83
4	From	-	41	48	50	47	46	47	47	48
	To	-	65	69	72	73	74	76	78	78
5	From	-	48	50	53	50	50	50	49	50
	To	-	70	72	73	74	75	76	78	78
6	From	-	45	50	54	50	50	49	49	48
	To	-	70	71	73	72	73	74	75	76
7	From	-	45	48	53	50	51	50	50	49
	To	-	68	69	71	71	72	73	74	75
8	From	-	42	48	53	51	51	50	50	49
	To	-	69	70	71	71	71	72	73	73
9	From	-	43	46	52	50	52	51	51	50
	To	-	69	70	71	71	72	73	73	74

Chart 3: Gammonless Windows for Redoubling to 4

A Needs		1	2	3	4	5	6	7	8	9
					B needs					
2	-	-	-	-	-	-	-	-	-	-
	-	-	-	-	-	-	-	-	-	-
3	From	-	-	50	69	79	87	90	94	93
	To	-	-	75	82	85	89	91	94	94
4	From	-	-	31	50	65	75	82	86	87
	To	-	-	60	67	74	80	84	87	88
5	From	-	-	31	46	50	54	59	64	65
	To	-	-	61	66	74	79	83	86	87
6	From	-	-	26	42	46	50	55	60	61
	To	-	-	61	67	72	76	80	84	85
7	From	-	-	22	36	41	45	50	55	56
	To	-	-	56	63	68	72	77	80	82
8	From	-	-	16	29	36	40	45	50	52
	To	-	-	51	57	63	68	73	77	79
9	From	-	-	17	29	35	39	44	48	50
	To	-	-	53	58	64	67	71	75	77

Doubling when you are two away

Compare the top rows of windows in Charts One and Two, showing the double and take points for 2-away cubes. At these scores, if the leader doubles, the trailer has an immediate automatic redouble to 4, because the extra points are of use only to him. Thus all these doubles have wastage for the leader.

Will the doubler invariably take the recube? We've never seen one correctly passed, but it is a possibility. The unfortunate doubler may have some disastrous anti-joker lurking in the dice cups which wrecks his position at a stroke. Or he may be doubling from a backgame because a potentially market-losing quadruple shot has popped up, knowing he'll have to pass the recube on his four misses; that is, if the opponent doesn't elect to play on for the gammon!

We can verify from Chart One that the automatic recube makes for some **high doubling points**:

- 67% at 2 away/3 away.

- 77% at 2 away/4 away.

- 70% at 2 away/5 away.

Chart Two shows the windows which apply at the start of the game, when each side has the normal 25% gammon expectancy. As we should expect, these windows are even narrower than their Chart One counterparts, because the possibility of winning the match with an uncubed gammon deters the double. Now the doubling points are:

- 71% at 2 away/3 away.

- 81% at 2 away/4 away — add a few more wins and there won't be a window at all; in other words there will no correct double/takes.

- 78% at 2 away/5 away. (Note that the taker has a lower take point here than before because he gets a little value from his own gammons on the 4 cube.)

The same logic would seem to say that **take points** will be low, for the automatic recube appears to be giving the taker such superb value. But this isn't necessarily the case. Looking at the same Chart One windows, the respective take points (remember that we derive these by subtracting from 100) are:

■ 25% at 2 away/3 away (appreciably higher than for money).

■ 18% at 2 away/4 away (certainly lower than for money); and

■ 22% at 2 away/5 away (about the same as for money).

Why the variation?

■ At 2 away/3 away both players have wastage on the 4 cube.

■ At 2 away/4 away the 4 cube is ideally efficient, exactly winning the match.

■ At 2 away/5 away, the 4 cube gets the trailer to Crawford game 1 away/2 away — not quite so glittering a prize.

And why aren't the take points lower? The reason is that that doubler is also getting extra value for his cube. Remember: the point(s) which win the match or get to the Crawford game are always worth a lot more than the ones which don't.

What conclusions can we draw about these scores? If we have reached a stage in the game by which gammons have been either greatly reduced or eliminated, then we may well have a correct double-in or even a cash.

But what do we do in positions such as the following two?

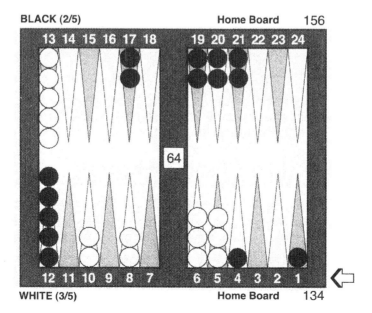

Diag. 69

Diagram 69 shows a very routine position at 2 away/3 away; Diagram 70 a more challenging position at 2 away/5 away.

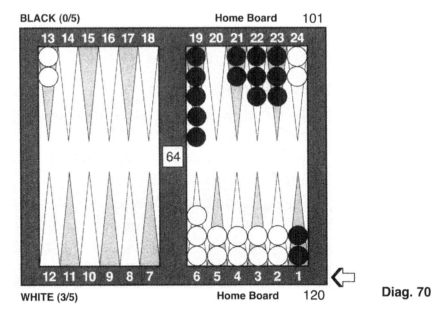

Diag. 70

For money, Diagram 69 is a big pass and Diagram 70 a fairly close take. At the score, not only are these both takes; neither is a double. The gammon fractions for the leader are not in either case massive — 15% in Diagram 69, 21% in Diagram 70. But they are the crucial factor.

The leader mustn't double these sorts of positions, because:

(a) The undoubled gammons get him to the winning post.

(b) A cube kills those gammons, rendering them no better than plain wins.

(c) If things go awry later on, but the cube hasn't been turned, the leader simply loses a single point and remains not only alive but ahead in the match.

Too Good but Not Good Enough

Here we have a paradox which is often seen when one side needs two points, though it is not in the least unique to this score. The potential doubler is simultaneously Too Good to Double (he wants to get maximum value for his gammon) and Not Good Enough (unlike in a money Too Good situation, the opponent here should take).

Too Good/Not Good Enough is a situation generated when the potential doubler has a powerful gammon threat and the take (which doesn't need to involve an automatic recube) will either kill or devalue those gammons. Note that if we tweak these positions to increase the wins enough for the potential doubler to overshoot the cashpoint, he now has a Double/Pass; only if we tweak very generously does he become just plain Too Good and correct to play on for the gammon.

Let's look at an example which arose in a match of Lamford's in an apparently unlikely match situation:

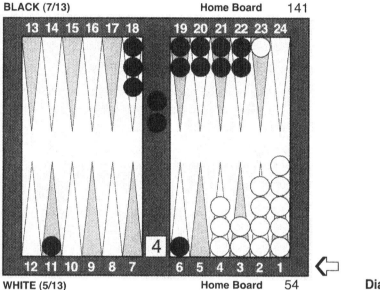

Diag. 71

The player on roll is Too Good/Not Good Enough and mustn't double; and the opponent's take is easy — plenty of wins here. If the roller loses on the present 4-cube he is still clinging to life in the match at 8 away/2 away. This is worth 13%, the match equity chart tells us. Be aware that this is much preferable to a poke in the eye with a sharp stick: it is a big mistake to discount this sort of equity in match backgammon, thinking 'Well, I'll never win from that score.' You will … 13% of the time!

On the other hand, if the roller doubles and loses on the 8-cube, he'll be out of the match altogether.

But the key concept is that the roller mustn't kill his own gammons. At present they are ideally efficient, getting him exactly to the winning post. If he cubes, they will become worth nothing at all. Here the roller is only a small favourite to win the game; but over 70% of these wins are gammons.

Doubling when the Opponent is two away

Some of the most insidious backgammon myths, the hoariest misconceptions you will hear tournament players relate, derive from the over-generalised notion that match leaders should play conservatively but trailers must be bold.

In fact, some players wrongly believe that you should play aggressively in money games but cautiously in match play. This makes sense only if a significant skill difference makes it reasonable for the better player to try to avoid giving the weaker player any chance to get lucky, avoiding at all costs big cubes, gammonish takes and suchlike.

The notion of playing conservatively when leading and boldly when trailing might seem intuitively plausible. But consider the following position:

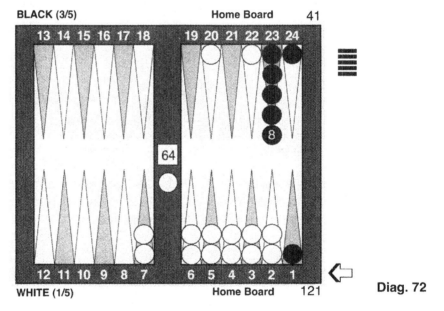

Diag. 72

No doubt of course that the trailer's double is correct here. What about the take? The leader has five checkers off and we know from *Starting Out in Backgammon* (page 104) that this makes these kinds of positions typically takes for money. But the position gives the trailer some serious extra vig compared to standard close-out positions: aces to hit a second checker from the bar (11/36 rolls) to become a huge favourite. He may be able to recreate this threat even if he misses first time.

Clearly quite a big pass for money. But readers may be surprised to learn that at 2 away/4 away it rolls out as a narrow take, even though the leader can pass and still lead 2 away/3 away. In fact the take point (18%) and the winning chances here (19%) are approximately the same, and the position is just on the take side of the borderline. Most players would wrongly pass this like a shot; many wouldn't fancy accepting the cube even if the ace-point blot were covered.

One important general lesson which can be learnt from studying Chart One is that the match leader can take boldly if there are no gammons — and it is the trailer, not the leader, who must be conservative with the cube. Once again, the governing principle is that the points which win the match have extra value.

In the following position we have the same scoreline. The trailer has opened with a 3-1, and in reply the leader has rolled 6-3 and run into the outfield 24/15.

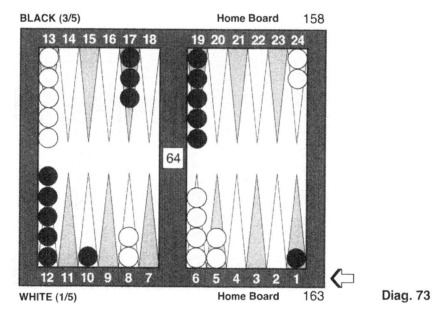

Diag. 73

Only the maddest steamer would double this position for money — there are not nearly enough market-losing sequences — but at the score it's not so clear. Even after just two moves the trailer has considerably boosted the 25% average expectancy of winning a gammon, and at a score where a doubled gammon would win the match with perfect efficiency.

The position was extensively discussed after it arose in a doubles match in the late 1980s involving some of the strongest players in America. The trailers doubled and the leaders passed. Nobody seems previously to have thought it could possibly be even a double; Neil Kazaross, the recipient of the cube, amazed everyone by concluding it was actually a pass!

Subsequent analysis argued that both the double and the pass were correct, and Roy Friedman (who'd cubed the position) later published a persuasive argument, in his magazine *Leading Edge*, to the effect that splitting to the bar and playing 13/10 would have given the leaders a take. We now know that both analyses were in fact wrong. It is the double that is questionable (Snowie 4 can't make up its mind) — the take is crystal clear; and running is the better play.

Nonetheless, even the possibility that this early position might be a correct double shows the immense potency of trailer gammons at scorelines like 4 away/2 away and (to a slightly lesser extent) 3 away/2 away, 5 away/2 away and so on. The trailer should be considering doubling very early if he significantly improves his chances of winning a gammon.

A final example, this time at 3 away/2 away:

Here the trailer has made no new home-board points, whereas the opponent now has four; nor does the trailer have a particularly good distribution of builders. But he has an anchor, has put two checkers on the bar, and has a terrific attack. He will lose lots of games but win plenty of gammons whenever his

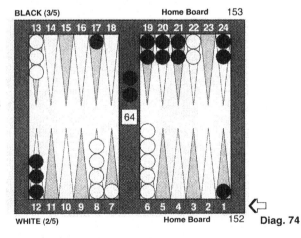

attack doesn't break down. For money this is no double. But even though gammons aren't as efficient at the score as they would be at 4 away/2 away (because of wastage, one of the extra points can't be used), this volatile position is already a clear pass at the score.

Exercise 16: A four-part question. What are the cube actions in the following position for each of the situations stated:
a) 2 away/4 away in a match; cube centred as shown?
b) 5 away/3 away in a match; White owns a 2-cube?
c) Money game; cube centred as shown?
d) Money game; White owns a 2-cube?

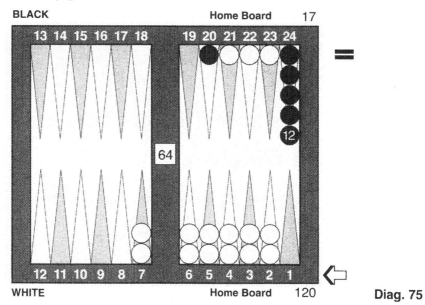

Diag. 75

Exercise 17: How do you play in the following position, a) at DMP? b) 2 away/1 away Crawford? c) 1 away/2 away Crawford?

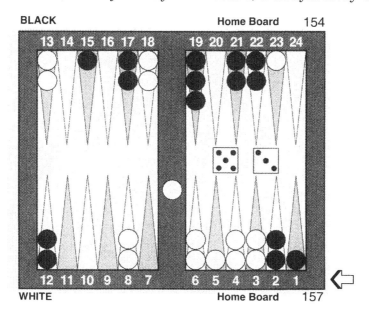

Diag. 76

Chapter Eight

Advanced Cube Handling

- **When to Double: Volatility**
- **When to Take: Efficient Recubes**
- **Recube Windows**
- **High Cubes and Skewed Scores**
- **The Gammon Value Chart**
- **Points to Remember**

When to Double: Volatility

Should we double (or take) whenever we think we're in our doubling window?

If only life were so straightforward! Look, for example, at the Windows Chart One on page 82 showing the gammonless initial doubling windows and find the box for the particularly subtle and interesting scoreline 3 away/4 away. This is a window of positively department-store dimensions, stretching fully 40 percentage points, opening at 38% and closing at 78%.

Goodness, the startled reader might exclaim, I can even double the starting position! That idea is absurd — but why, exactly?

Let's take another look at the position in Diagram 58, repeated here for convenience. If we were ever to get so far in the game without a turn of the cube, this position is a correct 3 away/4 away double/take.

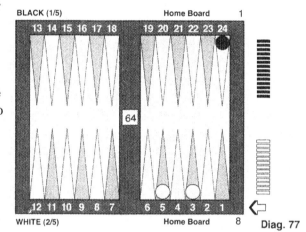

BLACK (1/5) Home Board 1

13 14 15 16 17 18 | 19 20 21 22 23 24

64

12 11 10 9 8 7 | 6 5 4 3 2 1

WHITE (2/5) Home Board 8 Diag. 77

This claim should amaze the uninitiated. It seems so illogical. White is ahead in the match, and this is the last roll of a game in which he is most definitely not the favourite. He wins on only 14 of his numbers and misses with the remaining 22. An opponent who would double this for money is a friend to cultivate; it is a huge beaver. White is nothing but a snivelling underdog here, with 39% winning chances.

Yet this is a marginally correct cube at the score! How do we explain this counter-intuitive result?

■ Black can never use the cube because if White misses, Black is gin (backgammon jargon for certain to win).

■ If White wins he gets to the Crawford game.

■ If White loses he is only a slight underdog in the match, at 3 away/2 away, with equity of 40%.

■ This is the last roll of the game. White would prefer to be doubling somewhere much higher in his window. But there won't be a future doubling opportunity: it's now or never.

Note that we should also double this if we were leading 2 away/4 away. This time the window given in Chart One doesn't apply, because the recipient of the cube never gets to make the normal automatic redouble, and the worst that can happen to White is that he finishes up tied at 2 away/2 away.

How does this differ from money play? In a money game we should double or redouble last-roll positions if we have an advantage, however small (Diagram 60 on page 66 shows the minimum possible correct money cube). Only in match backgammon are we ever correct to make underdog doubles.

There's an important caveat, however. In match play you should only make such marginal doubles in zero-skill positions against opponents whom you consider to be of equal or greater ability; not against any duffer you happen to meet. Knowing that you stand the best chance of beating a poor player if you can grind out a long match, you should avoid trusting too much equity to the caprice of the dice gods. In addition, steer clear of high cubes and gammonish positions against weak players!

Same score. This time a middle-game position. Does the leader have an 'action double' here?

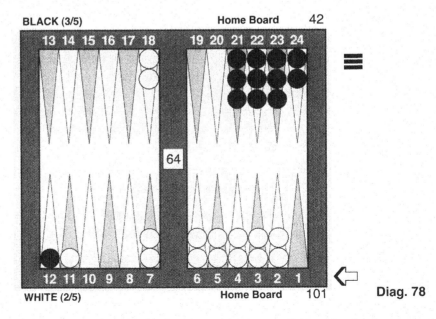

Diag. 78

We have 17 hitting sixes but 19 missing non-sixes, so once again we're the miserable underdogs. There are next to no gammons. And this isn't a last-roll position.

Or is it? In fact the position behaves in just the same way as the previous one. The key characteristic they share is sky-high volatility. If we do hit, we badly want to have doubled:

■ The two points will take us to the Crawford game.

■ It's now or never. If we hit, we lose our market massively.

■ When we miss and are immediately doubled out, we retain 40% match equity, as we did in the earlier position.

As a result, failing to double this position is almost a blunder.

Finally, same score, this time a holding game:

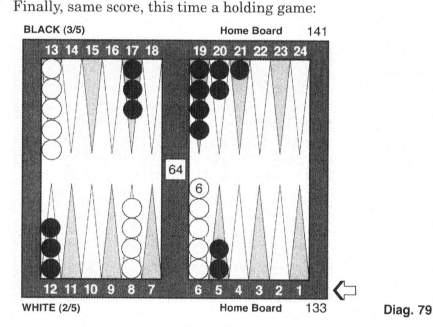

Diag. 79

Far better winning chances here, but now there is very little volatility. We lose our market with 6-6, 5-5, 4-4 and 3-3; otherwise we'd be pleased to have waited. Not quite a double.

The vital general point is this: in money play and match play alike we would like to be able to double at the precise point at which the cube is so efficient that we are indifferent as to whether our opponent takes or passes. But our dice are seldom obliging enough to take us to that ideal point. Accordingly we generally double **low** — maybe a third of the way up our window — when the position looks volatile. It may be a six-rolling contest to jump a prime or that we are shooting at a target; at any rate, something very good may happen so that we suffer a big market loss. Conversely, we will double **high** in our window, maybe two-thirds of the way up, when we have a low-volatility position like a holding game or race. **On average we need to be about halfway up our window to cube**.

When to Take: Efficient Recubes

So the decision to double depends on (a) knowing the window and (b) estimating the volatility.

Deciding whether we can take match cubes is more complex. First of all, some of the take points given in the charts above are **absolute**; others need to be interpreted in the light of recube possibilities.

The take points are absolute values if there can be no further correct use of the cube or if there is a recube which is completely automatic. For example, the 25% take point at 3 away/2 away assumes we are always making the automatic recube. We can **always** take with winning chances of 25% or better. But the recube at a score such as 4 away/3 away is anything but automatic. If the taker could never use the cube, the take point would not be the relatively low 22% given in Chart One on page 82, but a much higher figure.

Let's do a risk-reward calculation to work it out. White is offering an initial cube at 3 away/4away:

a) Black can **pass** to trail 4 away/2 away, match equity **33%**.

b) Black can **take and win** to lead 2 away/3 away, match equity **60%**.

c) Black can **take and lose** to trail Crawford 4 away/1 away, match equity **18%**.

So — ignoring the potential recube — the take nets a **reward** of (60-33) = **27%** when Black wins, but runs a **risk** of (33-18) = **15%** when it loses.

From the formula: Take point = Risk/(Risk + Reward), we get a much higher take point than the 22% given by the chart: 15/(15 + 27) = 36%.

Those windows in the chart which show a take point which is not absolute assume that the cube is completely **live**. What does this mean? It is that they not only factor in recube vig —

they do so assuming that if the taker gets a recube it is always the most efficient possible — that fabulous cube right at the cashpoint, so perfect that the lucky doubler is indifferent as to whether it's taken or rejected.

The figure we have just worked out makes the opposite assumption: that the cube is unusable to the taker — in other words, completely **dead**.

In real life we would correctly expect that take point lies somewhere between these two extremes. But where? Take the following position, a pure race at 3 away/4 away in which the leader is 100-111 ahead.

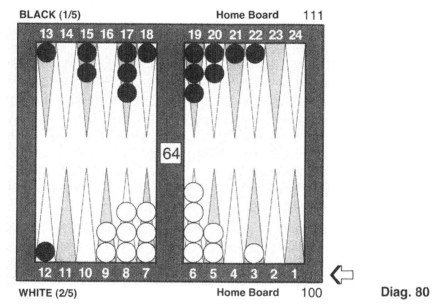

Diag. 80

We know from *Starting Out in Backgammon* (pages 48-49) that this is a money double/take and can work out, using the equation given in this book on page 10, that Black's winning chances are around 25%. We know from the discussion above that this must put us easily high enough in the very wide window at this score to double.

Is this enough to take? We've done all the maths but this has provided us with only the possible range of take points — here anything between 22% and 36%.

This is where, once again, volatility is relevant. We can justify taking close to the theoretical minimum take point in relatively non-volatile types of games like holding games and races, because they are the games most likely to give efficient redoubles near to our cashpoint. On the other hand, when the position is volatile, our recubes are likely to be inefficiently early or late; they are therefore less valuable to us, and we require better winning chances to take a cube.

A good rule-of-thumb for races is to assume the take-point is about one-third of the way between the lowest and highest figures we have calculated. We would therefore use 27%, as this is about one-third of the way between 22% and 36%. So even in a race, the 25% game-winning chances we have here are not quite enough and the rollouts confirm the pass.

Recube Windows

Chart Three on page 83 shows what a very different animal the match recube is from the money recube. For money, the value of cube ownership (holding exclusive rights to the use of the cube) normally makes us wait for a bigger advantage when we recube than we require to make an initial double. In match play, denying our opponent access to the cube may still be a big consideration, but a much bigger factor in short matches (or close to the end of longer ones) is the altered balance of risks and rewards. Are we getting to the Crawford game or winning the match on the recube? Are we activating or killing the opponent's gammons?

You should pay particular attention to some of the most surprising windows, such as the recube windows at 4 away/ 3 away and 4 away/4 away. Why are the cashpoints so low at these scores? The answer is that in both cases our opponent's take point is the same as her equity if she passes — 40% and 33% respectively. There is a simple principle to remember when your opponent doubles or redoubles and the match is on the line for both of you if you take: you should accept the cube if your winning chances in the game equal or exceed your match equity if you pass.

Be aware also that these recubes kill all gammons. You have effectively arrived at double match point.

High Cubes and Skewed Scores

There is a tendency to avoid doubling when we have a big lead, but the correct method is exactly as before: we use risk-reward equations to find out the doubling point and/or the take point.

Take the position opposite in which White is 5 away/11 away and owns a 4-cube. Lamford took a little while here to redouble to 8, and his grumpy opponent in a British Isles Backgammon Association tournament took umbrage and

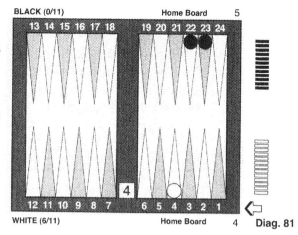

BLACK (0/11)　　Home Board　5

WHITE (6/11)　　Home Board　4　　**Diag. 81**

commented: 'Who are you trying to kid?' as he angrily rejected the cube. Lamford resisted the temptation to correct the 'who' to 'whom', but did point out that the take was easy.

Before we work out the doubling window, we have to consider what happens if White rolls 2-1. Black will clearly redouble to 16. But what about White's take of the 16-cube? Despite the fact that White wins $^{11}/_{36}$ or 30% of the time, White has to pass the recube, as he thereby retains 35% winning chances in the match at 6-8 down, which is better than playing the position for the match with only 30% chances. Therefore:

a) If Black passes, he trails Crawford 11 away/1 away, match equity 3%.

b) If Black takes, then whenever White rolls 2-1, Black can win with the cube and lead 3 away/5 away, match equity of 65%.

Black's **risk** is therefore 3% and his **reward** is 62%; thus he has a take point of 3/(3 + 62) which is about 4½%. As he is winning whenever White rolls a 2-1 (5½%), he should take.

What about the double? One of its disadvantages is that White does not get another roll if he misses, whereas, if he keeps the cube, he does. However, we cannot generalise with cube decisions. Let us work out the risk-reward ratio for White.

a) If he doubles and wins, his match equity is **100%**.

b) If he doesn't double and wins, he leads Crawford 1 away/11 away, match equity **97%**.

c) If he doubles and loses, he will trail 5 away/3 away, match equity **35%**.

d) If he doesn't double and loses he leads 5 away/7 away, match equity of **62%**.

So White's **risk** is **27%** (62 – 35) and **reward** is **3%** (100 – 97). The **risk-reward ratio** is 27/(27 + 3) which is **90%**. This gives a doubling window for a last-roll 8-cube of 90-95%. White is winning 94% of the time after doubling, and therefore, despite the release of the cube to Black, it is a blunder not to double.

The Gammon Value Chart

The key to successful match backgammon is the accurate appraisal of the value of your gammons and your opponent's, both on the present cube and after a possible cube turn.

We have seen how we can learn or calculate match equities and derive doubling windows to guide us to correct decisions. But gammons tend to make windows very hard indeed to work out.

How, for instance, could we assess this position, first for money and then at the score given?

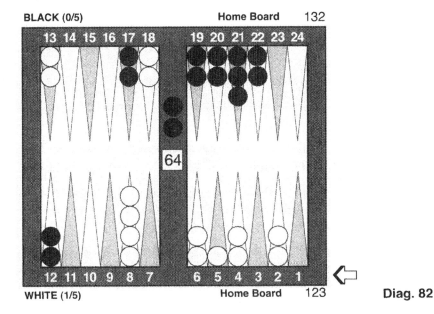

Diag. 82

White has a powerful blitz, with two Black checkers on the bar against a 3½-point board, but Black has good compensation with her 4-point board and a gammon threat of her own if she can turn the game around. For money this is a double and quite a clear take. To pass would give up the equivalent of a tenth of a point.

Gammon Values at Different Scores in a 5-Point Match

B Needs

A Needs	Post 1			Crawford 1			2			3			4			5		
	1	2	4	1	2	4	1	2	4	1	2	4	1	2	4	1	2	4
2	-	0.00	-	1.00	-	-	0.83	0.00	-	0.97	0.00	0.00	0.79	0.00	0.00	0.84	0.00	0.00
3	-	1.00	-	0.02	-	-	0.74	0.45	0.00	0.83	0.49	0.00	0.93	0.43	0.00	0.55	0.44	0.00
4	-	1.02	-	0.57	-	-	0.41	1.00	0.00	0.57	0.98	0.00	0.64	1.00	0.00	0.52	0.84	0.00
5	-	0.60	-	0.03	-	-	0.39	0.70	0.45	0.44	0.73	0.33	0.48	0.80	0.22	0.48	0.58	0.22

How to use the chart: As in the Match Equity Table and Windows Charts, the vertical axis gives the points needed by A and the horizontal axis gives the points needed by B. The numbers 1, 2 and 4 denote, respectively, a centred cube, a 2-cube and a 4-cube. The figure 0.84 in the top row, for example, is the value of A's gammons on a centred cube when leading 2 away/5away.

At the score, however, this is a clear pass. This makes sense: a doubled gammon wins the match. But how much better if we could quantify exactly what our match gammons are worth.

Fortunately we have a powerful over-the-board method for doing this. The chart on the previous page, like the Windows Charts, is calculated from the match equity table. This time our figures indicate the values of gammons at different scores and on different cubes. This allows us to compare them both to one another and to the familiar benchmark of the value of gammons for money.

What exactly do we mean by the 'value' of a gammon (sometimes confusingly referred to as the gammon 'price' in backgammon literature)? Once again, we are making a comparison between a **reward** — winning a gammon and its associated **risk** — losing the game. In a money game if we own a 2-cube and play on for a gammon instead of cashing the game, we hope to gain the reward of an extra two points (we win four instead of two points), but we risk turning the two-point win we might have had by cashing into a two-point loss, a difference of four points. In other words, for money the cost of losses (assumed for the sake of simplicity to be single game losses) is twice the benefit gained by winning gammons. We need to be winning two gammons for every extra loss to justify playing on, and the 'value' of gammons is therefore 0.5.

So far so good. But we know that the value of points won and lost at match scores is not a constant figure and this implies that the value of gammons will be different at every single match score and for every single cube. The Gammon Value Chart gives these values for all possible cubes in a 5-point match. Ambitious match backgammoners are recommended to memorise as much as possible of this invaluable information. However, if we know or can work out the relevant match equities these values shouldn't be too hard occasionally to calculate at the table.

How are gammon values calculated? Let's revisit a scoreline we've looked at in detail on pages 88-89: 4 away/2 away. At this score, 2-cube single wins get the trailer to equality, 50% match equity at 2 away/2 away. Gammon wins make his equity leap another 50% to a match-winning 100%; if he loses he blows 50% and finishes up with 0% and a hard luck story. Thus gammons at this score are no longer worth the modest 0.5 they rate for money, but a whole 1.0.

If we had the choice we would always prefer to know our doubling windows. But what an effective alternative tool this chart is. Returning to the Diagram 82 decision on page 100: the 2-cube gammon price of 0.84 confirms the impression that this is a big pass at the score. In a similar way the chart points us to the correct solution to the Diagram 61 question on page 70: the 36% improvement (relative to their money worth) in the value of our gammons when we double at 5 away/5 away turns the money take into the match score pass.

These are crucial numbers by which the practical player can steer a course in match backgammon.

Points to Remember

Finally, a summary of some of the most essential guidelines to sound match play:

a) Play aggressively and aim for an early double when you need four points.

b) Try to make an advanced anchor and get a quiet holding game when your opponent needs four points.

c) When you need two points, try to play for an undoubled gammon (unless your opponent also needs two points).

d) If your opponent needs two points, look to double earlier than usual, as you give her a dead cube and kill her gammons.

e) Fight to stop your opponent getting the point that takes her to two, four, six or eight points from victory. Tend to concede a point that takes her to three, five or seven points away.

f) A race is the best type of game when you own the cube. You don't have to worry about gammons and it is a lot easier to do the match equity calculations.

g) Don't vary your play too much. 90% of checker plays are the same regardless of the score.

h) If the take/pass or double/no double calculation comes out very close, then consider the skill of the opponent. If you are in danger of being gammoned by a weak player and the position is not complicated (i.e. you can't trust the opponent to mess it up), then be inclined to pass. Initial doubles against weak players in races are close to normal, but redoubles can introduce some distortion. In essence, avoid high cubes against weak players, and try to avoid their lucky redoubles from hopeless races.

Exercise 18: What would the cube actions be at the following scores — and why:

a) 4 away/2 away? b) 2 away/4 away? c) 3 away/4 away?

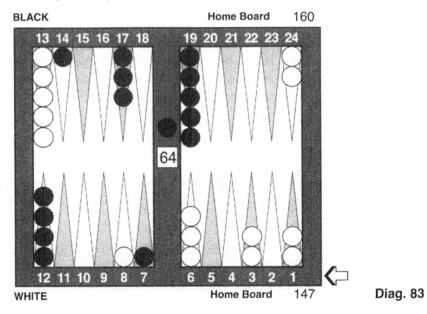

Diag. 83

Exercise 19: In the following position, what are the correct cube actions at the given score?

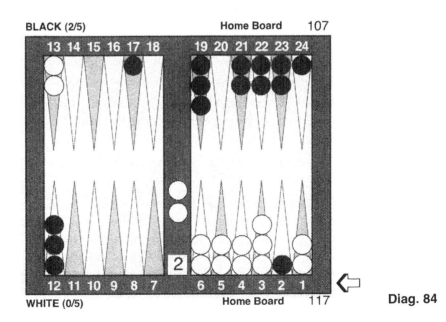

Diag. 84

Part Three

Technology

by Stefanie Rohan

Chapter Nine

Computers and the Internet

■ **Playing on the Internet**

■ **Playing and Analysing on Computers**

■ **Internet Sites**

■ **Suppliers**

Computers offer a variety of ways to improve your game, as well as opportunities to play for fun or money. Indeed, some people play most of their backgammon on the internet. The computer resources available fall into several categories:

Playing on the Internet

In this category there is now an almost bewildering variety of servers, both free and fee-charging. The first (it just celebrated its tenth anniversary) and, in the author's opinion, the best, is FIBS (First Internet Backgammon Server). You will always find a great many people from all over the world on FIBS: (**www.fibs.com).** Unlike the other playing sites listed here, FIBS is simply a server, and does not come with its own interface. However, there are several good interfaces available. The two most popular ones are Beggar's Backgammon Terminal for Windows (**www.gamercafe.com**) and MacFIBS for Macintosh (**www.fibs.com/macfibs**). These are both shareware, with registration fees of $30 and $20 respectively.

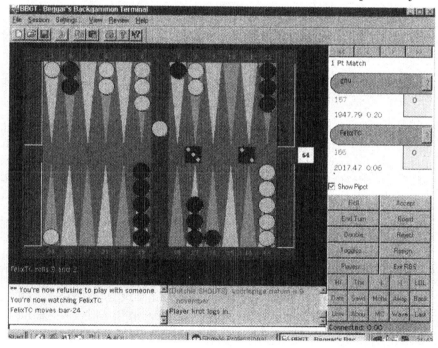

The BBGT Interface for FIBS

A good free alternative for Windows is 3DFIBS found at **www.anzwers.org/free/3dfibs**. This program also offers the opportunity to play against Gnu Backgammon (see below). There is also a Java client for FIBS, which can be found at

www.fibs.com/~cthulhu, and information about still more interfaces is available on the FIBS home page.

FIBS does not offer money play, and it does not provide tournaments in 'real-time'. It does have a league and tournaments — see **http://fibsleagammon.free.fr/**. David Escoffery also runs a twice-yearly money tournament.

'Real-time' tournaments can be played on a number of free and pay sites. All of the paid servers offer either a free trial or guest membership which allows you to try out the server with some of the features removed. The conditions on a few sites are not ideal — the reader may run into problems, such as the inability to 'undo' checker moves or to resign gammons; others have annoying adverts, inconvenient checker-movement commands, or the necessity to search graphically and find a table with one player sitting at it in order to get a game.

The best advice for the reader is to try out a number of sites until you find one with features and an interface that you are comfortable with. Another important factor is how many people are online when you are trying to get a game. Here is a list of some of the more popular online backgammon servers:

Free Sites

FIBS (**www.fibs.com**): Featured above in detail.

MSN Zone (**http://zone.msn.com/backgammon**): There were over 5,000 players on line when we sampled it but the majority were social players. The site is recommended if you have a friend starting out in the game, but we found the board to be low-contrast and the procedure for joining games a bit clumsy.

Playsite 3.0 (**www.playsite.com**): A well-organised site with frequent tournaments and around 150 online when we logged in. Players are very friendly and the site had a sense of being a club with lots of extra features such as photos and profiles.

Yahoo (**www.yahoo.com**): A two-tier system, but more functional than some for free members. Tournament and ladder play, however, require a subscription. There were over 1,500 online when we visited.

Game Colony (**www.gamecolony.com**): A few hundred players, but the java applet was too slow on our admittedly not state-of-the-art PC. The server also offers low-stakes money play with a rake of 10% of winnings.

Winner Zone (**www.winnerzone.com**): This site offers low-stakes money play but with a 20% commission on winnings, which is too high. Unsurprisingly, there was no-one playing when we dropped in.

TrueMoneygames (**www.truemoneygames.com**): The new kid on the block which has a lot of top players including leading German experts Dirk Schiemann and Ralf Jonas. There is no annual subscription and the site is supported solely by the commission on money games and matches.

Pay Sites

GamesGrid (**www.gamesgrid.com**) A site used by most top players, including Nack Ballard, Jerry Grandell, Kit Woolsey and Paul Magriel. You can play for money or just for rating points, and regular tournaments are organised. There are many jackpot tournaments and a lot of money games with the commission varying depending on the stake. Beware of the occasional shark with an artificially deflated rating.

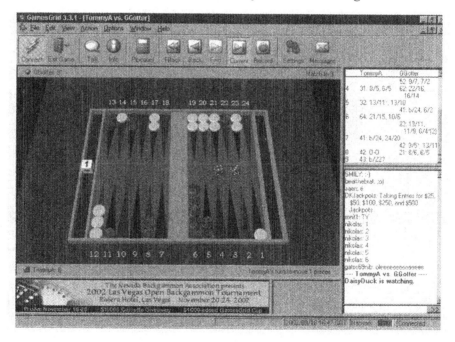

The 3D option on the Games Grid interface

Netgammon (**www.netgammon.com**) A high number of French and Turkish players among the 20,000 members. The standard is not as high as GamesGrid. We experienced a couple of bugs in the software which the owners are now addressing.

VOG (**www.vog.ru**) A lively site where you can play exotic variants such as Longgammon, Narde (Fuega) and Crazy Narde (Gul Bara). There are a huge number of tournaments in all forms of the game, some with entry fees and prizes. The 100% return on all entry fees and all money games, at the time of writing, is a big plus. Friendly players, including many South Americans, and lots of stats and pictures.

Playmaker (**www. playmaker-world.com**) A popular site, and now the home for those that used to be on the free site Funcom, which closed its backgammon server in 2002. Very professional software and regular tournaments.

World Game Site 2000 (**www.gamesite2000.com**) An ambitious multi-game server. There were some reasonable players but the standard was below that of Games Grid.

The above sites have annual subscriptions ranging from around $20 per year to $80 per year, and you should check all aspects of the site before joining, to make sure it is suitable.

The site's rake is a very important consideration when choosing a money-play server. For instance, Games Grid and TrueMoneygames have commissions which are generally similar but vary according to match length and stake.

Online tournaments, with $25 entry fees, are organised by the site at **www.redtopbg.com/RWG**. You are sent the pairing and arrange to play on a server of your choice.

The first dedicated money-play server Backgammon4Money (**www.backgammon4money.com**) is now defunct but still solicits deposits even though it has left a trail of unpaid customers across the world. It now does not answer emails.

Another type of backgammon is the turn-based server — postal backgammon! Its Your Turn (**www.itsyourturn.com**) and Daily Gammon (**www.dailygammon.com**) are two popular sites. On these servers a player will typically enter a number of matches or tournaments at once, and play a move in all of them every day or so when logged on. For most this may be too slow, but many enjoy the leisurely pace and the opportunity to chat with other players without the need to make a move quickly.

An interesting variant of backgammon is Tric Trac in which online tournaments are held on **www.playmaker-world.com**. For details of these events subscribe to the mailing list via **www.backpacker-backgammon.com**.

One other site worth a visit is **www.gammonzone.com** which organises top quality matches, on Microsoft Zone, at which spectators are welcome.

Playing Computers and Analysing

Playing against a computer opponent and analysing matches can be discussed together, because the best programs for these functions do both. The two most popular player/analysers are Jellyfish (**http://jelly.effect.no**) and Snowie, now in its fourth version (**www.bgsnowie.com**). Both of these programs come in several versions. Jellyfish offers its Light version (player only) as freeware, along with the previous release version of its Player version. Snowie is more expensive and has a few more bells and whistles. A particularly good feature is the ability to analyse or roll out an entire match or session in one operation, so that you can then take another look at the moves it disagreed with; with Jellyfish it is necessary to look at each move in turn for analysis or rollout.

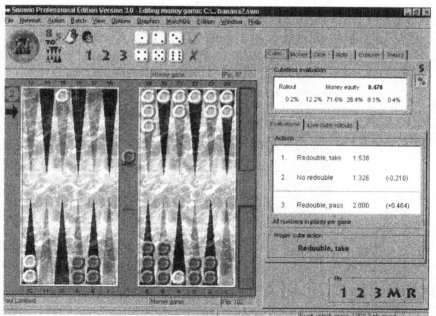

The detailed Snowie Interface

Another program, BGBlitz, has been recently issued and details are on the site at **www.bgblitz.com**. Here there are also some free downloadable matches in a database.

Gnu Backgammon (**www.gnubackgammon.com**) is a good free alternative to these programs; gnu is a strong player and analyser. Its interface is a bit clumsy. An excellent free program called Blowfish (**http://fibs.com/~blowfish**) uses the same engine with a more 'Snowie-like' interface. Blowfish is the analyser, and Snowfish is its associated playing program. Monte Carlo is a good free program that plays one-point matches. It can be downloaded from **www.gamercafe.com**. Many of the above programs are also 'members' of playing sites. Gnututor1 plays on FIBS, and will give you hints!

Internet Sites

The net surfer with an interest in backgammon may well be aware of most of the top sites already. Art Grater's amazing portal at **www.back-gammon.com** is a good place to start. Another fine site is the Chicago Point Links page at **www.chicagopoint.com/links**, which categorises sites by their main purpose, for example servers, suppliers or clubs. **www.gammoned.com** is another information site with excellent links to clubs worldwide. Both contain a calendar of major tournaments. **www. gammonitis.com** has details of events run by the new UK organiser Liz Barker. Michael Crane of BIBA runs monthly UK tournaments and Carol Joy Cole has a complete list of US events (see below for both). Finally, the site at **www.bg-info.com** has good photographs and links.

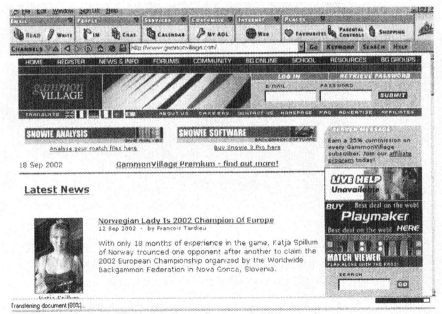

The excellent Gammon Village site

The free Mind Sports Olympiad site at **www.msoworld.com** still has many articles but the backgammon pages are rarely updated. Gammon Village at **www.gammonvillage.com** has regular interesting features including a lively forum. Kit Woolsey's site at **www.gammonline.com** has frequent useful theoretical articles and interesting positions. Both these last two charge a subscription but are good value for money.

Suppliers

Many suppliers of equipment, books and software also have sites on the internet. Some recommended ones are:

Carol Joy Cole, Flint Area Backgammon Club, 3719 Greenbrook Lane, Flint, MI 48507-1400 USA; tel/fax: (810) 232 9731; email: cjc@tir.com; web site: **http://.homepage.interaccess.com/~chipoint/cjc.html**

Michael Crane, BIBA, 2 Redbourne Drive, Lincoln LN2 2HG; tel: (+44) 1522 888676; email: info@backgammon-biba.co.uk. web site: **www.backgammon-biba.co.uk**

David Naylor, tel: (+44) 930 460647 produces high-quality leather boards. View them at **www.backgammon-boards.co.uk**. Email: dnaylor@globalnet.co.uk.

For hand-made wooden boards, we recommend Harry Bhatia, 92 Barrowell Green, London N21 3AY. Tel: (+44) 208 886 8286.

Martin de Bruin, Publisher, *European Backgammon News*, Suite 6/202, P O Box 561, 1/5 Irish Town, Gibraltar; tel/fax: (+34) 950 133009; email: backgammon@wanadoo.es

A&K Klassische Spiele, Grüner Weg 14, 34117 Kassel, Germany; web site: **www.shopit.de/ak_spiele/frame-e.htm** Sets and boards for all classic games.

Backgammon Shop, Dansk Backgammon Forlag ApS, Gersonsvej 25, DK-2900 Hellerup, Denmark; tel: (+45) 3940 1785; fax: (+45) 3940 0144; email: ct@bgshop.com; web site: **www.bgshop.com**.

The last-named has many out-of-print titles, but the best source of rare books and old backgammon boards on the internet is the auction at **www.ebay.com**. The site at **http://boardgamecentral.com/games/bg.html** has a useful directory of suppliers.

Bibliography

The following books, in approximate ascending order of difficulty, are recommended reading :

Starting Out in Backgammon by Paul Lamford
Backgammon by Paul Magriel
Backgammon for Winners by Bill Robertie
Backgammon: An Independent View by Chris Bray
What Colour is the Wind? by Chris Bray
501 Essential Backgammon Problems by Bill Robertie
100 Backgammon Puzzles by Paul Lamford
Backgammon for Serious Players by Bill Robertie
Backgammon with the Giants: Neil Kazaroos by Antonio Ortega and Danny Kleinman
Jerry Grandell: His Most Important Matches by Antonio Ortega and Danny Kleinman
Classic Backgammon Revisited by Jeremy Bagai
World Class Backgammon Move by Move by Roy Friedman
Advanced Backgammon, vol. 1 and 2 by Bill Robertie
New Ideas in Backgammon by Kit Woolsey and Hal Heinrich
Fascinating Backgammon by Antonio Ortega
Can a Fish Taste Twice as Good? by Jake Jacobs and Walter Trice
Funny Thing Happened on the Way to the Four-Point by Jake Jacobs
How to Play Tournament Backgammon by Kit Woolsey
Cubes and Gammons Near the End of the Match by Antonio Ortega and Danny Kleinman
Boards, Blots and Double Shots by Norman Wiggins
In the Game Until the End: Post Ace-Point Games (revised ed.) by Bob Wachtel

Backgammon Today is the best magazine on the game and a subscription can be booked at **www.backgammon-today.de** or from Playmaker AG, Am Borsigturm 50, 13507 Berlin, Germany. email: info@backgammon-today.de. Another good book which is worth looking out for in second-hand bookshops is *Backgammon for People Who Hate to Lose* by former World Champion Tim Holland. You might also enjoy the excellent books by Danny Kleinman which, like all the above books, should be available from the suppliers on page 113.

Solutions to Exercises

1. The race is 100-104 and no adjustments are needed. Using our formula from page 10 we get the winning percentage $P = 50\% + (900 + 100 + 1600)/(100 + 28 + 25)$. This works out to 67%. The rollouts gave around 66%. Our formula is good enough to diagnose the big pass at this score, with the take point of 40% as explained in Chapter 5.

2. White has three surplus checkers on the ace-point, for which we add two pips each, two surplus checkers on the deuce-point, incurring a one pip penalty each, and a four-gap, getting a four-pip penalty. The three gap is not a problem here, as threes can be played from the 'heavy' six-point. White also has an extra checker, so we add another two pips. Black merits a one-pip penalty for the sixth checker on the six-point. One other point is that three doubles bear off four checkers for White while only one does for Black, and we therefore need to deduct half a pip for each working double. Adding the penalties gives an adjusted pip-count of $59\frac{1}{2}$-$67\frac{1}{2}$, which is a lead of 8 pips and a clear pass (our formula gives 79%). This is confirmed by the rollouts with White winning 81% of the time.

3. The correct play for money is the sharp 7/3* 24/23. This offers excellent winning chances on the 16 dances, although the hits from the bar could well lead to a gammon. At any score where gammons count extra for the opponent, such as 2 away/4 away, we should play safe with the ugly 8/4 5/4. It should be noted, however, that this does not solve all our problems, and after the passive play we can still be gammoned.

4. Again we are weighing up the risks of a bold play against a safe play. We are behind in the race, and Black is threatening to run away. At DMP the aggressive play with 8/5* 8/7 is correct. Black may still crash if she enters with a deuce, and we are well-placed if she dances. In a money game, it is correct by a bigger margin to play 8/5* 8/7, which loses fewer gammons despite leaving 20 shots! Picking up one blot with 8/5* 2/1 is second choice, but this makes it much harder to cash the game when the opponent rolls badly.

5. Although Snowie 4 thinks this is a strong double, we think it is mistaken. Black has a lot of compensation on the other side of the board, and White has only 9s and 11s (plus small doubles) to put a second checker on the bar. Even then White will lose his market only if Black dances, and not by much. However, if Black anchors, White regrets doubling, as he will become the underdog. Most of the time White gets a strong double next roll, and a systematic analysis of the 1296 possible rolls and replies confirmed this view.

6. The solid 23/17 13/10 is correct, at money by the small margin of 0.02 but at double match point by over 3%. Hitting two checkers with 10/4*/1* increases the number of gammons, but at the cost of converting too many single wins into losses. Black has a four-point board, and don't forget that an aggressive play needs to gain twice as many gammons as the number of additional losses it incurs. Making the bar with 13/7 10/7 is just wrong here – if Black anchors on our four-point she will then be in great shape.

7. We need to sort the possible next rolls for each side into three groups and estimate the equity for each:

a) White stays out with 16 rolls. This occurs 44% of the time.

b) White hits a checker with 20 rolls and Black anchors with one of her 13 rolls. This occurs $20/36$ x $13/36$ = 20% of the time.

c) White hits a checker with 20 rolls and Black stays out or enters without anchoring with 23 rolls. This occurs $20/36$ x $23/36$ = 36% of the time,

Of course, the above are sweeping generalisations. White might hit two checkers, or Black might hit back from the bar. These factors look as though they should roughly cancel out.

Each of these variations is very difficult to estimate, but let us make a stab at the task:

a) It looks clear that Black has a redouble, but it should be evident that White has an easy take. Black still has to cover both blots. Let us estimate –0.4 for White here on our six-tier method from zero to one.

b) After White hits and Black anchors, it looks like White would be redoubling anyway and Black would surely be taking with a high anchor and a strong board. Let us go for +0.4 for White, on the same approach as in a).

c) After Black dances (or enters without anchoring), White is obviously too good as over half his wins are gammons, albeit with a few losses. We are looking for an equity between 1 and 2. Hard to judge, so let us guess 70% gammons, 20% single wins and 10% losses — an equity of 1.5 on a one-cube.

We now multiply the equities in a), b) and c) by their chance of occurring. We get (–0.4 x 0.44) + (0.4 x 0.2) + (1.5 x 0.36).This gives an overall equity of 0.45. With such high volatility this looks like a redouble/take, and the cubeless equity of 0.49 in the rollout confirmed this. In such a complicated position, we would only attempt to evaluate the cubeless equity and then apply a general rule for doubling and taking.

8. Crushed positions are often misunderstood, but this is an easier position in which to estimate the equity than exercise 7. There are two distinct variations:

a) White hits with 20 rolls.

b) White breaks his 5-prime with 16 rolls.

On the 20 hits, White will be a big favourite and Black would then have a clear pass. By how much? Well it doesn't look Too Good, as Black still has her deuce-point game, but we wouldn't dream of taking, so let's go for +0.8 for these.

On the 16 numbers that break the prime, it is not clear who is favourite. Both sides have a four-prime, but Black may not tidy up. She might get an ace, however, and make a 5-prime. If we don't know who is favourite, we should estimate zero for these rolls.

Overall our estimate of the equity is therefore (20 x 0.8)/36. We do not need to include the rolls with an equity of zero. This gives an equity estimate of +0.44. The rollouts gave a figure of +0.52 and confirm the Redouble/Take. Perhaps we underestimated a bit the variations where White hits both Black checkers and gets some gammons.

9. To estimate the equity of this position we should consider:

a) The 14 rolls which hit on Black's four-point.

b) The 9 rolls which dance.

c) The other 13 rolls which enter without hitting.

The first thing we should notice is that if we do not hit we will be doubled out, whether the cube is in the centre or on our opponent's side. We thus know the equity of both b) and c) both after doubling and after not doubling. It is –2 and –1 respectively. What about after hitting? Well, if we have not doubled we will have no alternative but to cash the game, as the Jacoby Rule prevents us from winning a gammon until we have doubled. If we have doubled, however, we will win a lot of gammons. How many? We will probably escape and put maybe three of the opponent's checkers on the bar, and if we apply the method on page 50 we get an estimate that 85% of our wins are gammons. This looks an overestimate though, as we may lose a home-board point before jumping the four-prime, or we may only hit one further checker. Let us go for 75% gammons. After the 14 hits we will win say 90% of the time — even after being closed out the opponent can win after bearing off, and before we reach the bear-off we have to jump that pesky prime. This gives us, on the 14 hits, after doubling:

Single wins 22%; Gammon wins 68%; Losses 10%.

This gives us an equity of $(2 \times 0.22) + (4 \times 0.68) - (2 \times 0.1) = 2.96$ on a 2-cube, which we will round up to 3. We can thus work out our equity over 36 sample games after doubling. It is about $[(3 \times 14) + (-2 \times 22)]/36 = -2/36$. What is the equity if we do not double? That is easy; we win the 14 hits and lose the 22 misses, so it is $(14 - 22)/36 = -8/36$. Clearly we should double, as our equity is increased, and equally clearly Black should beaver, as her equity is positive. However, that only doubles our $-2/36$ to $-4/36$, still much better than the $-8/36$ by not doubling. Snowie 3 and 4 both easily diagnoses the correct double/beaver. This is the so-called Kauder Paradox, named after the player who first discovered this type of position.

10. The first task here is to break down the different types of games and assign a percentage to each; we may make errors, but they will only affect a portion of the games. What types of games are there?

a) White hits and Black does not anchor. Clearly very bad for Black and an obvious pass. Usually Black will get two checkers closed out, sometimes three. We use the rough estimate of −0.8 on a one-cube for a huge pass. As there are 20 hits and 25 dances in response, this variation occurs 39% of the time.

b) White hits and Black anchors. A clear take for Black, and I wouldn't be sure of the double. Let us estimate −0.4 for these. There are 20 hits and 11 anchoring responses — so this line occurs 17% of the time.

c) White doesn't hit in Black's board. He will try hitting on his ace-point hoping to be hit back, but Black may stay out. Even if White has to close Black out without catching another checker, he will still be favourite, as Black has only seven checkers borne off. From our table on page 48, we know that White is around 55% in these lines, but we should increase this to 65% to allow for the chance of still picking up a second checker. This would give an equity of −0.3 (0.35 − 0.65). This variation occurs in 16 of the 36 rolls: 44% of the time.

If we multiply each equity by the chance of the variation occurring we get an overall equity as follows:

$$(−0.8 \text{ x } 0.39) + (−0.4 \text{ x } 0.17) + (0.3 \text{ x } 0.44) = −0.51$$

The equity of −0.51 is cubeless, and represents an easy take, as there will be some games where Black gets an effective 4-cube. This was confirmed by the rollouts, which gave a cube-owned figure on a 2-cube of −0.94 for Black. We can usually take with a cubeless equity of −0.55, sometimes lower, depending on the value of the cube to the taker.

11. a) At 3 away/3 away we can pass and be 40% in the match. If we take and lose we will be 25%. So our risk is 15%. If we win we will be 75%. So our **reward** is 35%. This gives a take point given by Risk/(Risk + Reward), which is 15/(15 + 35) = 30%. However, this doesn't consider the potential recube for the taker, and we have seen that a reasonably accurate method to find the **effective** take point is to deduct one sixth from the figure we calculate. This gives a take point of 25%.

b) For a recube at 3 away/3 away, we are putting the match on the line, so we need to calculate only our equity if we pass. We will be 3 away/1 away, which is 25%, so this is our take point.

c) At 4 away/5 away we can pass and be 50%. If we take and lose we are 4 away/3 away, which is 43%. (Older charts give 41% here — they underestimate the powerful cube potential for the player 4 away, both with gammonish initial cubes and with recubes). So we **risk** 7%. If we take and win, we are 2 away/5 away, which is 74%. Our **reward** is 24%. Our take point is therefore 7/(7 + 24) = 23%. Deduct one sixth and we are down to 19%. Surprisingly low.

d) This is relatively easy. If we pass we are 11 away/1 away Crawford, which is 3%. If we take and lose, that is it, so our risk is a mere 3%. If we take and win, as we will have redoubled immediately, we will be all square at 3 away/3 away, match equity of 50%. So our reward is 47%, and our take point is thus 3/(3 + 47) which is 6%. No need to deduct one sixth here, we have already allowed for the recube!

12. a) Let us look at the different possibilities. If we double and she passes, her equity is 18% at Crawford 4 away/1 away, so clearly she should take, as she has the 28% chance that we roll one of our 10 missing numbers. What about our double? Some readers might think: 'I am going to be Crawford anyway; why put the match on the line?' But let us do the maths. If we don't double and lose we have 40% match equity. If we do double and lose, it is all over — 0% match equity. So we **risk** 40%. If we double and win we are 100%, so our **reward** is 60%. Our doubling point is therefore 60/(60 + 40) = 60%. We are winning this position 72% of the time, so we do much better to double — unless the opponent is a very weak player, in which case we should avoid such a big swing on one roll.

b) A different ball game. Our opponent can pass and retain 40% winning chances in the match at 3 away/2 away, or play this position with a tad under 28% winning chances instead. It is clear that we should double and she should pass.

13. a) At 5 away/5 away our opponent can pass and retain 35% winning chances. If she takes and loses she will have only 15% match-winning chances, so she risks 20%. If she wins, she goes to 85%. So her reward is 50%. Her take point is therefore 20/(20 + 50) = 29%. As she is only winning the position 28% of the time, she has a borderline pass.

b) At 5 away/8 away our opponent can pass and trail 8 away/ 1 away Crawford — a mere 6%. If she takes, she wins the match 28% of the time — an obvious take. But, what about the double? If we don't double and lose, we get to 5 away/4 away, which is 42%. If we double and lose we are 0%. So our **risk** is 42%. If we don't double and win we are 94%, so we only get another 6% as a **reward** for our douhle. So our doubling point is 42/(6 + 42) = 88%. Clearly a big error to double!

c) 8 away/8 away. An easy one. Black can keep 26% winning chances by passing and playing 8 away/4 away, so she should do this, and we do not need to do any further calculations: Double/Pass.

14. The correct play is 3/o 1/o. By getting down to six checkers, White is very likely to save a whole roll in bearing off his remaining checkers, considerably increasing the chance of a gammon. Although the aggressive play increases the losses from virtually zero to over 10%, there is a greater increase in the number of gammons. At this score, as we will see from the

Chart on page 101, we should make any play which converts more single wins into gammons than it converts single wins into losses. The gammon value at this score is one, about as high as it ever gets, compared with the normal gammon value for money of one half.

15. Although we are not concerned about being gammoned, we should still make the advanced anchor with 24/20. Black is well placed to attack on her five-point, and making the anchor makes us a small underdog, while making our own five-point is 0.04 worse.

16. We have a triple shot which will make us a huge favourite here, but if we miss, there is a big risk of being gammoned. How do we think about the position? Let us look at each situation in turn:

a) **2 away/4 away with the cube centred**.
If we double and win the game we go to 100%, whereas if we do not double and win the game we will be 85% at 1 away/4 away, so we gain 15% by doubling. However the downside is large. If we miss, our opponent will not be making her customary 'automatic' redouble — which we would pass like a shot — but rather play on and try to gammon us, which she will achieve maybe half the time. We drop to 50% or 0%, depending on whether we get gammoned. Doubling here is a big blunder as Black can use all four points with perfect efficiency.
No Double/Take.

b) **5 away/3 away in a match; White owns a 2-cube.**
If we don't double and win we will be 50% in the match whereas if we double and win, we will go up to 75% at 1 away/3 away Crawford. If we don't double and lose we will either get gammoned and lose the match, or retain 15% chances at 5 away/1 away Crawford. If we double and lose, the match is over, whether or not we get gammoned. So we have a clear double, gaining 25% and only risking an average of 7.5%. What about Black's take? She can pass and be all square in the match at 3 away/3 away. If she takes and wins she wins the match with or without a gammon, so she goes to 100%. If she takes and loses she is 3 away/1 away Crawford, which is 25%. So the **risk** is 25% (50 – 25) and the **reward** 50% (100 – 50), a take point of 33%. As she is unlikely to win on the 27 hits, it is clear that she does not have that, so the cube action is:
Redouble/Pass.

c) **Money game; cube centred.**

Although White is winning around 70% of the time cubeless, and the position is extremely volatile, only one side can win a gammon. Therefore White should not double in a money game, as he would thereby activate gammons for his opponent. White does better by cashing on all the 27 hits and giving up on the nine misses, an overall equity of (27– 9)/36, which is exactly 0.5. If White doubles, Black will obviously take. White now wins only about 90% of the hits and gets gammoned on around half of the misses (he has 12 crossovers against 13 to get off the gammon). Thus White's equity after a double and a take is about [(0.9 x 2 – 0.1 x 2) x 27 – (0.5 x – 4 + 0.5 x –2) x 9]/36 which works out at about 0.45. So **No Double/Take**.

d) **Money game; White owns a 2-cube**

Unlike variation (c) where the cube is centred, White can still be gammoned on his nine misses, as, unlike (c) the cube has already been turned. It is now a blunder not to redouble — an example of the rare Latto paradox in which a position is a redouble but not an initial double. This position is duck soup to Snowie 4 which easily diagnoses the Latto. The equities on the rollouts were 0.42 after a redouble/take and 0.34 after no redouble. Of course these need to be multiplied by 2 — the current level of the cube — so the real equities are +0.84 for doubling (on a 4-cube) and +0.68 for a centred 2-cube. **Redouble/Take**.

17. a) The correct play is to make our five-point with 8/5. The game has a long way to go, and we are not worried about the gammon threat on the other side of the board. Second choice, however, is making the anchor, with hitting (18/15*) a distant third. If we already had our 5-point, hitting would be correct.

b) When we need a gammon it is even more imperative to make our five-point. Again hitting trails in third.

c) This time avoiding the gammon is the biggest priority. Making the solid anchor with 23/20 is best by some margin over the second choice of making our five-point.

18. a) At 4 away/2 away the position is not far from being Too Good to Double. Readers should have no trouble working out that the pass is massive. About 55% of White's wins are match-winning gammons.

b) At 2 away/4 away the position exemplifies the Too Good/Not Good Enough paradox. This time White wants to win the match with an undoubled gammon. By doubling White would kill his own gammons. If cubed, Black should take like a shot. Her take point is very low — 18% — and this sort of blitz position always offers lots of wins for the defender — about 34% here. **No Double/Take**.

c) At 3 away/4 away there will be wastage on doubled gammons, and a subsequent recube by the opponent would kill them. Snowie 4 misassesses this as a marginal double, whereas it is in fact **No Double/Take**.

19. This position has much in common with Diagram 59, not least in the scoreline and the value and position of the cube. If we can understand this one we should be able to understand the earlier one.

White's situation looks far more dire here. A lazy player, seeing that the position is neither clear nor immediately appetising, would be likely to shrug and roll the dice. After all, he is trailing 5 away/3 away in the match, has two checkers on the bar against a 4-point board, and stands in obvious danger of being closed out and gammoned.

But we've seen that in match backgammon even underdogs should bark and snarl in the right circumstances. Consider:

- The effect of plain wins and losses. On the present cube, the underdog only equalises when he wins. And when he loses, he cringes like a whipped cur at Crawford game 5 away/1 away (match equity: 15%).

- The effect of gammon wins and losses. Roughly 50% of each player's wins are gammons. If the trailer doubles, despite wastage (he can use only one of the four extra points) he still gets a lot more value (0.22, The Gammon Chart on page 101 tells us) for it than we might think, because this is the point which wins the match. On the other hand, the cube-turn kills his opponent's gammons.

- Volatility is astronomical, so it's another now-or-never situation. White's aces, preferably followed by Black's dancing, lose the market good and proper, making White favourite to win a gammon. (5-5 is also not unwelcome!)

So the discouraging cubeless money equity — minus 0.41, monster beaver! — is an irrelevance. Match and money play really aren't the same game and the underdog must seize the moment for a remarkable redouble.

Glossary

This glossary contains all the terms the player will meet in this book, together with many of the colourful expressions the player will encounter if playing backgammon socially or in tournaments.

Anchor A point in the opponent's home board, or the opponent's bar-point, occupied by two or more of your checkers.

Automatic Double By agreement in a money game only, if both players roll the same number on the initial roll, the cube is automatically placed on two, but remains centred.

Backgame A position in which we have two or more anchors in the opponent's board and aim to hit a shot as she attempts to bring her checkers into her board.

Baffle Box A device into which dice are thrown when rolling. It contains a helter-skelter of three slopes which ensures that the roll is fair.

Banana Split A loose hit inside our home board achieved by breaking an existing point and thereby creating two new blots.

Beaver To double the value of an offered cube while retaining ownership of the cube on our side of the board.

Blitz An attack on one or more of our opponent's back checkers with the aim of repeatedly sending them to the bar.

Box In a chouette, the player who is on his own.

Boxes (in US, Boxcars) A roll of double sixes.

Broken Prime A prime with a gap in it.

Builder A spare checker, usually on one of the points from a player's 11-point to his seven-point, which can be used to make a point in board on a future roll.

Captain In a chouette, the member of the team who takes the final decision on checker plays.

Cash A double that should be dropped; it is also implied that it is not correct to play on for a gammon.

Centred Cube One that has not yet been turned in that game, and shows 64, although its real value is one.

Chouette A form of money game in which one player (the box) plays against other players (the team) one of whom (the captain) is rolling and making the checker plays. Each player has his own cube and makes his own decisions whether to take or pass.

Cocked Die A die which has not come to rest flat in the player's right-hand side of the board or which is on top of a checker.

Contain To prevent one or more checkers from escaping from our side of the board by a combination of making blocking points and hitting.

Count To add up the number of pips required to bear off all the remaining checkers; the total so reached for both sides.

Crash To be forced to break the six-point and possibly other points in our home board; also termed to **crunch**.

Crawford Rule In tournament matches only, the rule by which, in the game immediately after one player reaches a score one point from victory, the cube may not be used.

Cube The doubling cube, which starts in the centre of the board and which may be used by either player to increase the value of the game.

Cubeless A game (or rollout) conducted without the cube in play, for example at double match point.

Cubeful A type of rollout, or the equity resulting from such a rollout, in which the cube actions at each roll are considered.

Dance To fail to enter from the bar.

Deuce A roll of two on a die; the two-point is also known as the deuce-point.

Direct Shot Any situation where a blot is six or fewer pips away from an opponent's checker.

Diversification Placing our checkers such that the maximum number of rolls will play well on the next throw.

Double Any roll of the same number on each die; any offer of a cube; to offer the cube.

Doubling Point The minimum percentage required at that match score to make a correct offer of the cube.

Double Match Point (DMP) A situation in a match in which both sides need one point for victory and the cube is not used.

Double-in A double that should be taken.

Double-out A double that should not be accepted; the same as a cash.

Duplication A situation where one or more of the opponent's rolls offers a choice between different hitting, escaping or point-making moves, thus reducing the number of good rolls which the opponent may throw.

Equity The average expected amount that will be won or lost in that particular game. For example, if we are certain to win a backgammon, our equity is +3.

Fan American slang for failing to enter from the bar.

Flunk More American slang for failing to enter from the bar.

Free Pass A situation in a match, post Crawford, where the leader can drop a cube without any reduction in his match winning chances.

Free Take A misnomer for the converse situation, where the leader should accept an initial cube with very low winning chances.

Gammon Value Often called the gammon price, the ratio of the value of gammons to losses at a particular score.

Golden Anchor The opponent's five-point; our 20-point.

Golden Point Our five-point.

Golden Triangle The optimal bear-off structure for a pip-count of 70.

Hit Loose To hit a blot in our home board, thereby giving our opponent an opportunity to hit the same checker from the bar.

Holding Game A situation in which a player has an anchor and is waiting to get a shot or to run with a double.

Indirect shot Any situation where a blot is seven or more pips away from an opponent's checker, and there is at least one roll of the dice which will allow the opponent to hit it.

Jacoby Paradox A position in the bear-off, with one side having a checker on the five-point and two-point, which is not a double if the opponent will offer you a takeable cube when we miss, but is a double if the cube is of no value to our opponent if we miss.

Jacoby Rule The rule, usually employed in money games, that a gammon or backgammon does not count until an initial double has been made.

Janowski Formula A formula for calculating the match equity at a given score. It is $P = 50\% + 85\% \times D/(T+6)$ where D is the difference between the two scores and T is the number of points required by the trailer to win the match.

Kauder Paradox A rare position which is a correct double and a correct beaver. It can apply only in a money game.

Kleinman Formula A method of estimating winning chances in a race by looking up values in a chart for D^2/S where D is the lead in the pip-count and S is the sum of the two pip-counts.

Latto Paradox A very rare position, only in a money game, which is a correct redouble but not an initial double.

Lipped Cups Cups that have a ridge at the top to prevent the dice being rolled in an unfair way by a mechanic.

Lover's Leap An opening roll of 6-5 played by moving a checker from the 24-point to the mid-point.

Match Equity The probability of each side winning the match at that score; it may incorporate the winning chances in a game in progress.

Mechanic Someone who can cheat by rolling the dice in such a way that certain numbers appear with a greater frequency than they should. Also known as a dice mechanic.

No Dice Slang for a faulty roll or for cocked dice.

On Tilt Losing very heavily and steaming, possibly doubling after the opening roll or beavering normal doubles.

Outfield Point Any point outside the two home boards.

Outside Prime A sequence of four or more points, none of which is in the player's home board.

Partner One of the players in a large chouette, usually the last person to lose, who has an equal share in the box and may confer or take separate cube decisions depending on local rules.

Pick and Pass To hit a blot with one part of the roll and to continue with the same checker to an occupied point, or off the board.

Pigeon Slang for a weak player who is prepared to play for money against stronger players.

Pip-Count The total number of pips which must be rolled to bring all checkers into the home board and to bear them off.

Post Crawford The stage of the match after the Crawford game has been won by the trailer.

Precision Dice Dice manufactured with extreme accuracy, which have no bias.

Premature Roll A roll made before the opponent has completed his play by picking up his dice.

Prime A sequence of at least four consecutive points, each occupied by two or more checkers of the same colour.

Rac(c)oon After an initial double has been beavered, to turn the cube to double its previous value, while allowing the opponent to retain it on his side of the board.

Race A position where all, or virtually all, contact has been broken and the possibility of hitting shots is minimal or non-existent.

Rake The percentage take from a money game, tournament prize fund or internet site, retained by the organisers.

Return A shot from the bar against one of the opponent's checkers immediately after you have been hit.

Rollout A means of evaluating the equity of a position by playing (or having a computer play) a large number of games from that position.

Settlement An agreement to end the game prematurely with a certain number of points being paid by one player to one or more others.

Shake To mix the dice using the dice cups prior to rolling; also used as a general term for any roll or throw.

Slot To voluntarily place a blot on an important point with a view to making that point if the blot is not hit.

Snake A rolling six-prime with a single checker caught behind it, usually resulting from a heavy backgame or an anti-computer strategy.

Snake Eyes A roll of double ones.

Split To move a back checker, occupying an anchor, one or more pips within the opponent's home board or to the opponent's bar-point.

Steaming Making irrational cube decisions in money games in a desperate attempt to recover previous losses.

Switch To move two checkers from one home-board point to another home-board point, hitting an opposing checker.

Take Point The lowest winning percentage for that match score at which we should still accept a double.

Timing A measure of how long one can retain a desired position before being forced to make concessions.

Tempo Play A hit of an opposing checker, often on our ace-point, for the purpose of taking away half the opponent's roll and thereby stopping her from attacking us.

Thorp Count A formula for evaluating winning chances in a bear-off which adjusts for gaps and checkers borne off.

Too Good A situation where our expectancy in a game is greater than the current value of the cube, and we should play on for a gammon

Trap Play To volunteer a direct shot with a view to forcing the opponent to move off an anchor.

Ward Count An improved race formula, similar to the Thorp count, but making better adjustments for distribution.

Wash A settlement where two or more players agree that no points will be won by either side in the current game. It normally occurs when the chances are approximately equal, and sometimes with a high cube.

Wastage In a match, points that we win in a game which are surplus to requirements for the purpose of winning the match. In a bear-off, excess checkers on lower points.

Weaver To deliberately make an inferior play, hoping to get our opponent to accept the cube incorrectly next turn. Named after the leading American expert Paul Weaver.

CPSIA information can be obtained at www.ICGtesting.com
Printed in the USA
BVOW09s0602051215

429411BV00004B/8/P

9 781857 443158